Principal Pipelines

A Feasible, Affordable, and Effective Way for Districts to Improve Schools

Susan M. Gates, Matthew D. Baird, Benjamin K. Master, Emilio R. Chavez-Herrerias

Commissioned by

For more information on this publication, visit www.rand.org/t/RR2666

Library of Congress Cataloging-in-Publication Data is available for this publication.
ISBN: 978-1-9774-0193-9

Published by the RAND Corporation, Santa Monica, Calif.
© Copyright 2019 RAND Corporation
RAND® is a registered trademark.

Cover images: Claire Holt/The Wallace Foundation.

Support RAND

Make a tax-deductible charitable contribution at
www.rand.org/giving/contribute

www.rand.org

Preface

The Wallace Foundation is committed to improving school leadership. To further this objective, it invested in the Principal Pipeline Initiative (PPI). The PPI supported efforts in six districts across the United States to develop principal pipelines through engagement in activities related to the preparation, hiring, development, evaluation, and support of school leaders. Policy Studies Associates (PSA) and the RAND Corporation conducted the evaluation of this initiative. Five prior reports by PSA document the PPI's theory of action and its implementation (Wallace Foundation, undated). A RAND report documents the resources and expenditures associated with the PPI (Kaufman, Gates, et al., 2017). This final evaluation report describes the implementation and effects of the PPI on student achievement, other school outcomes, and principal retention.

This report will be of interest to school districts, state education agencies, policymakers, and preparation programs around the country that are interested in school leadership as a lever for school improvement. It may be of special interest given expanded opportunities through the Every Student Succeeds Act (Pub. L. 114-95, 2015) to use federal funds to support initiatives to improve school leadership (Herman et al., 2017). The information in this report could help school districts and state education agencies identify investments in principal pipelines that federal funding could support.

This research was conducted in RAND Education and Labor, a division of the RAND Corporation, in collaboration with PSA. The work was funded through a subcontract from PSA to RAND on a contract between PSA and The Wallace Foundation. The study was funded by The Wallace Foundation, which seeks to foster improvements in learning and enrichment for disadvantaged children and the vitality of the arts for everyone.

RAND Education and Labor conducts research on early childhood through postsecondary education programs, workforce development, and programs and policies affecting workers, entrepreneurship, financial literacy, and decisionmaking. More information about RAND can be found at www.rand.org. Questions about this report should be directed to sgates@rand.org, and questions about RAND Education and Labor should be directed to educationandlabor@rand.org.

Contents

Figures

Tables

Text Boxes

Summary

Research across the decades has confirmed that effective school leadership is associated with better outcomes for students and schools. A high-quality school leader affects dozens of teachers and hundreds or thousands of students. It is a pivotal role.

Districts are a key lever for influencing the quality of school leadership. School districts hire school leaders, give them the important responsibility of running schools, and then support them in that role. Districts that seek to improve the quality of school leadership can draw on a solid base of research pointing to an array of effective school leadership improvement initiatives (see Herman et al., 2017). Leithwood et al. (2004) argued that "efforts to improve [school leader] recruitment, training, evaluation and ongoing development should be considered highly cost-effective approaches to successful school improvement" (p. 14). Yet there is an open question as to how districts can leverage this research base to support comprehensive leadership improvement at scale—so that high-quality school leadership is the rule rather than the exception.

This study examined the efforts of six urban school districts to put in place systematic processes for the strategic management of school leaders. We looked at what they were able to accomplish and what happened in schools as a result. The six districts were

- Charlotte-Mecklenburg Schools, North Carolina
- Denver Public Schools, Colorado
- Gwinnett County Public Schools, Georgia
- Hillsborough County Public Schools, Florida
- New York City Department of Education, New York
- Prince George's County Public Schools, Maryland.

Our findings show that such efforts undertaken by committed large, urban districts are feasible, affordable, and effective: feasible because each district was able to put the recommended processes in place, affordable because the cost was less than 0.5 percent of the district budget, and effective because of the resulting impact on student achievement.

What Happens When Districts Invest in Principal Pipelines?

The Wallace Foundation funded and provided technical assistance to the six districts listed above as part of its Principal Pipeline Initiative (PPI) from 2011 to 2016. The purpose was to examine whether a comprehensive principal pipeline would be more effective than business-as-usual approaches to the preparation and management of school leaders (Korach and Cosner, 2017). The term *principal pipeline* is shorthand for the range of talent management activities that fall within a school district's scope of responsibility when it comes to school leaders. The PPI organized these activities into four categories, referred to as *components*:

1. leader standards that guide all pipeline activities
2. preservice preparation opportunities for assistant principals and principals
3. selective hiring and placement
4. on-the-job induction, evaluation, and support.

In addition, the PPI districts were expected to develop systems to support and sustain these efforts beyond the timeframe of the initiative. For example, each district was expected to develop a database with information about current and aspiring principals called a Leader Tracking System.

This report documents what the PPI districts were able to accomplish. It complements a series of reports that presented findings from the evaluation of implementation of the PPI, a study describing the resources and expenditures associated with principal pipelines, and a study of the use of data systems to support this work. We considered how the districts changed policies, procedures, and practices, as well as the effect of those changes on student achievement, principal retention, and other outcomes, such as attendance, teacher perceptions of school climate, and teacher turnover. We also related findings about the effects of principal pipelines to what we know about pipeline implementation, including costs.

Objectives

Our objectives for this study were fourfold:

1. Describe what policies, procedures, and practices six urban districts were able to change when implementing principal pipelines and characterize the effect of implementation on those in the pipeline.
2. Estimate the school-level effects of the PPI on student achievement, principal retention, and other outcomes, including school climate, stakeholder satisfaction, and teacher turnover.

3. Explore the mechanisms through which effects are realized (e.g., whether particular components of the pipeline are most strongly related to effects).
4. Relate these findings to previously collected information regarding the costs of implementing principal pipelines.

Approach

To achieve these objectives, we

- documented how PPI districts changed policies, procedures, and practices over the course of the initiative
- examined the characteristics and experiences of newly placed principals in PPI districts over the course of the initiative, including the degree to which these principals were exposed to different components of the principal pipeline
- analyzed the outcomes of schools in PPI districts and compared them with outcomes of schools in other districts, focusing on comparing schools with newly placed principals to identify a "pipeline effect"
- analyzed the relationship between pipeline effects and exposure to specific components of the principal pipeline and school characteristics
- analyzed the relationship between pipeline effects and estimated pipeline costs.

The data sources for this study included the following:

- **District data on principals, schools and students.** PPI districts provided us with data on principals, aspiring principals, schools, and students, including demographic information, data on principal placement, principal exposure to pipeline components, and student-level achievement and other outcome data.
- **State data on principals and schools.** We obtained statewide data on principals and school outcomes, including school-level indicators of student achievement, student average demographics, and other student outcomes.
- **Survey data.** Policy Studies Associates (PSA) administered surveys to novice principals in 2013, 2014, and 2015 as part of its implementation evaluation efforts.
- **Expenditure reports from PPI districts and technical assistance providers.** Each participating district provided these to The Wallace Foundation on principal pipeline–related spending over the course of the initiative—from August 2011 through December 2015. Organizations that offered technical assistance to participating districts through The Wallace Foundation provided expenditure reports for their work to the foundation.
- **District proposals, budgets, and progress reports.** Each participating district provided these to The Wallace Foundation.

- **Interviews with district personnel.** PSA and RAND researchers conducted interviews with district personnel throughout the PPI as part of the implementation and resources and expenditure studies.
- **District personnel resource-allocation data.** RAND researchers collected these data to account for the value of the time that district personnel spent on principal pipeline activities.

We combined data sources and analytical approaches as described in Table S.1 to address four research questions aligned to the objectives stated above. We generated findings and synthesized those findings to develop our conclusions and recommendations.

To estimate the effect of the PPI, we compared changes in outcomes in PPI district schools with changes in outcomes in similar schools located in non-PPI districts in the same state.[1] Outcomes as of school year (SY) 2010–2011 served as the basis of comparison or baseline. The *PPI effect* is the degree to which the changes in outcomes relative to that baseline differed between schools in PPI districts (treated schools) and similar schools in the rest of the state (comparison schools). Comparison schools were selected not just from one or a few districts but from across the entire state. This gave us a bigger pool of comparison schools with newly placed principals and limited the chance that initiatives in any one non-PPI district would influence our findings. We approached our analysis from the perspective that other districts in the state were engaged in at least some of the pipeline activities and may have had initiatives related to specific activities but were not addressing all four pipeline components in a strategic way. The main effect we emphasize in this report focused on schools that received a newly placed principal in SY 2012–2013 or later—a time when the PPI efforts were in

Table S.1
Approach Used to Address Research Questions

Research Question	Data and Methods Used
What policies, procedures, and practices were districts able to change when implementing principal pipelines, and how did these changes affect pipeline participants?	Descriptive characterization drawing on Leader Tracking System, survey, cost study, and implementation study data
What was the overall effect of principal pipelines on key school-level outcomes, and how did these effects vary by district, cohort, and school characteristics?	Analysis of outcomes for schools with newly placed principals in PPI districts compared with outcomes for schools with newly placed principals in non-PPI districts using state data
Which components of principal pipelines are correlated with effects?	Examination of correlations between school-level effects and pipeline exposure
Are principal pipelines cost-effective? Which pipeline components appear to be most cost-effective?	Analysis of the relationship between school-level effects and pipeline cost estimates

---

[1] This approach is referred to as a matched difference-in-difference regression approach.

full swing. We also considered whether there was an effect of the PPI on all schools in PPI districts.

Scope

The study findings are most relevant to districts operating in similar contexts to the six large urban public school districts that participated in the PPI. All of the PPI districts

- were among the 50 largest school districts in the United States
- served more than 80,000 students and operated more than 130 schools
- were "minority-majority" districts, serving a student population that was somewhere between 65 percent and 96 percent minority, depending on the district and school year
- had demonstrated a commitment to school leadership improvement and had undertaken some efforts related to principal pipelines prior to the launch of the initiative.

While the lessons we derived from this study are most readily generalizable to other large urban districts that view school leadership as a strategic lever for school reform and have the capacity to implement pipeline components, the findings may also be of interest to

- districts that have not yet made a commitment to school leadership as a lever to promote school improvement
- districts that are smaller than the PPI districts but still play a role in managing school leaders—on their own or in collaboration with other districts
- charter management organizations that manage a cadre of school leaders
- state education agencies, principal preparation programs, and policymakers in other organizations.

Findings

The PPI was designed as a set of systematic, mutually reinforcing reforms to the way school districts manage the preparation, placement, and support of newly placed principals. Our multiyear study of this initiative in six large urban districts shows that such reforms are feasible, effective, and affordable. Our key findings are summarized in Text Box S.1.

Text Box S.1. Summary of Key Findings

The work is feasible.

- PPI districts were able to implement all components of a principal pipeline at scale.
- PPI districts approached pipeline enhancement in different ways depending on their starting point, needs, and opportunities.

The work is effective.

- After three or more years, schools with newly placed principals in PPI districts outperformed comparison schools with newly placed principals by 6.22 percentile points in reading and 2.87 percentile points in math. These statistically significant and meaningful effects imply that a school that received a new principal and whose students would otherwise have been at the median in reading achievement would have scored above the 56th percentile as a result of the PPI. We refer to this as the *main PPI effect* on achievement outcomes.
- Newly placed principals in PPI districts were 5.8 percentage points more likely to remain in their school for at least two years and 7.8 percentage points more likely to remain in their school for at least three years than newly placed principals in comparison schools. These statistically significant and meaningful effects imply that for every 100 newly placed principals, the PPI is associated with nearly six fewer losses after two years and nearly eight fewer losses after three years.
- We found statistically significant, positive effects of the PPI on achievement in elementary and middle schools and some evidence of positive effects for high schools.
- PPI effects on achievement were positive and statistically significant for schools in the lowest quartile of the achievement distribution and larger than for schools in the second-lowest quartile.
- PPI effects were positive and statistically significant in reading for five PPI districts and in mathematics for three districts. The PPI effect was negative and statistically significant in mathematics in one district.
- The three PPI districts that had the most room to grow on all components of the pipeline at the start of the study had positive PPI effects on achievement.
- Across PPI districts, novice principals' ratings of their hiring, evaluation, and support experiences improved meaningfully between 2013 and 2015.

The work is affordable.

- PPI districts spent about $42 per student per year on pipeline activities during the initiative. The lowest-cost components were the development of leader standards and selective hiring and placement.
- The per-student costs of the PPI are small relative to the student achievement benefits, based on a comparison between the academic return on investment (ROI) for PPI and other educational interventions.

What drove these effects?

- The entire package of PPI components appears to have worked as a cohesive whole, much as it was designed to do. We found little evidence that individual components were uniquely correlated with larger or smaller effect sizes.

The Work Is Feasible: All Six PPI Districts Were Able to Implement Comprehensive Pipelines, and They Did So in Different Ways

It is feasible for committed districts to do this work. All six PPI districts made progress to improve the way they were doing the pipeline activities. They all had different starting points, faced different opportunities and constraints, and went about the work in different ways. As of SY 2010–2011, three of the PPI districts did not have any of the pipeline components fully in place. Two PPI districts had two components fully in place, and one district had three fully in place. By SY 2016–2017, three of the districts had all of the components fully in place. The other three districts had two or three components fully in place and the remaining component(s) partially in place. All of the PPI districts made progress in implementation from different starting points.

By SY 2016–2017, all six PPI districts had implemented a range of activities related to the strategic management of school leaders, purposefully choosing to engage or not engage in specific activities. All the districts had adopted leader standards and were using those standards to inform other components of the pipeline. They had all developed Leader Tracking Systems. They were engaging in strategic hiring and placement for principals, using data from Leader Tracking Systems and practical demonstrations of competencies in the hiring process. Each district had a district-run principal preparation program for its high-potential assistant principals and a partnership of some kind with one or more external programs of principal preparation. Each district continued to provide mentoring for novice principals and had a principal evaluation system that used the district's leader standards.

While these similarities are real, the districts had and used important flexibility to approach the pipeline activities in ways that made sense given their contexts and to adjust their strategies over time. PPI districts allocated resources across pipeline activities differently. Some put a greater emphasis on preservice preparation than others. Some devoted more resources to on-the-job support than others. Districts adopted different approaches to providing preservice and on-the-job support. For example, in crafting strategies related to induction support, some districts concentrated the support in the first year, and others spread it out over four or five years. Because there was so much variation in how PPI districts accomplished the work, their experiences do not provide a specific recipe for other districts with regard to each component.

The Work Is Effective: Our Analysis Suggests That the PPI Benefited Students and Schools

Our main analysis found positive effects of the PPI on a wide range of outcomes that school districts care about. Evidence of such positive effects was widespread.

Schools with Newly Placed Principals in PPI Districts Outperformed Comparison Schools in Reading and Mathematics

We found that schools in PPI districts that received a newly placed principal in SY 2012–2013 or later outperformed comparison schools by 6.22 percentile points in reading and 2.87 percentile points in mathematics three years or more after the arrival of the newly placed principal (see Figure S.1). The results are of a magnitude that is sizable: They suggest that a school that received a new principal and whose students would otherwise have been at the median (50th percentile) in reading achievement without the PPI instead would have reading achievement scores above the 56th percentile as a result of the PPI.

We found no other comprehensive district-wide initiatives with demonstrated positive effects of this magnitude on achievement. Stecher et al. (2018) found that the Intensive Partnerships for Effective Teaching initiative did not achieve its goals of improving teacher effectiveness or student outcomes in the districts that implemented it. An evaluation of New Leaders' Aspiring Principals program, which serves a subset of schools within districts, found that, after three or more years, achievement in schools that received a New Leaders principal was 3.26 to 3.55 percentile points higher in mathematics and 1.81 to 2.27 percentile points higher in English language arts than achievement in schools that received a new principal in the same district who was not a New Leader (Gates et al., 2019). These effects measures are based on district comparisons and apply to the subset of schools that receive a new principal who completed the Aspiring Principals program. The effects on achievement attributable to the PPI were

Figure S.1
In Schools in PPI Districts That Received a Newly Placed Principal, the Change in Student Achievement in Both Math and Reading Was Substantially Better Than in Comparison Schools

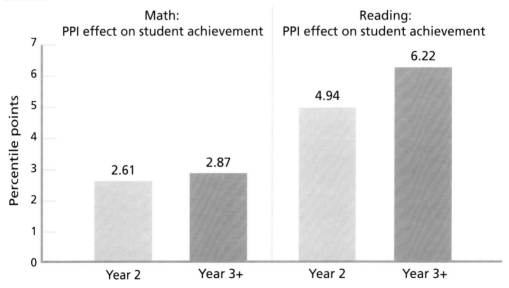

NOTES: The numerals indicate the *PPI effect* on student achievement: the difference between the percentile point change in achievement for schools in PPI districts and similar schools in other districts. The change in achievement is measured here between the baseline year (SY 2010–2011) and either two or three+ years after the placement of a new principal. These effects are statistically significant at the 5-percent level.

at least as positive as those found in recent studies of major district-led, district-wide initiatives focused on classroom teaching. For example, Teach for America, according to the U.S. Department of Education's What Works Clearinghouse, shows a 4-percentile-point increase in mathematics achievement and no distinguishable effect for reading, relative to comparison teachers (U.S. Department of Education, 2018c).

Newly Placed Principals in PPI Districts Were More Likely Than Comparison Principals to Remain in Their Positions

Our findings further indicate that principal pipelines had a favorable effect on the retention of newly placed principals, reducing the problems of school leadership churn in PPI districts. As shown in Figure S.2, newly placed principals in PPI districts were 5.8 percentage points more likely than comparison principals to remain in their school for two years and 7.8 percentage points more likely to remain in their school for three years. That means that for every 100 newly placed principals, PPI districts had nearly six fewer losses after two years and nearly eight fewer losses after three years. Two-year retention of newly placed principals varied by district and year ranging from 63 percent to 100 percent.

Figure S.2
Newly Placed Principals in PPI Districts Were More Likely to Remain in Their Schools

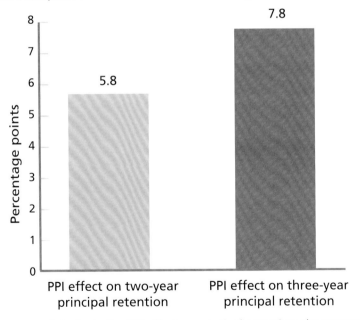

NOTES: The numerals indicate the *PPI effect* on principal retention: the percentage point difference between principal retention in PPI districts and similar schools in non-PPI districts. Retention is measured two and three years after the placement of a new principal. The effects here are statistically significant at the 5-percent level.

The PPI Benefited All Schools, Not Just Those That Received a Newly Placed Principal

We found evidence of positive, statistically significant, but somewhat smaller district-wide effects of the PPI on both mathematics and reading achievement in PPI districts. Overall, schools in PPI districts outperformed their comparison schools by 5.01 percentile points in reading and 2.29 percentile points in mathematics three years or more after SY 2012–2013.

There are a number of reasons why the initiative as implemented could have had a district-wide benefit—for example, through enhanced supervision and support for experienced as well as new principals or by allowing districts to identify and remove low-performing experienced principals. Additionally, districts selected to be part of the PPI had already implemented some of the pipeline activities prior to the 2012–2013 school year—so some principals who were new to their schools in years just prior to 2012–2013 may have had some experiences associated with pipeline treatment, such as induction support or exposure to preferred preservice providers.

District-wide effects could be due to other district initiatives not related to PPI in these six districts. We view this as unlikely, for several reasons. We are aware of no other factor that these districts had in common that would have likely contributed to the effects we measured in this timeframe. Statewide initiatives such as Race to the Top would have benefited comparison schools as well as schools in PPI districts. Major district-specific grants or initiatives, notably Intensive Partnerships for Effective Teaching, are unlikely to have contributed to the overperformance of PPI district schools relative to the rest of the state based on available evidence.

Positive Effects of PPI Were Widespread

We did subgroup analyses to assess whether the findings varied across districts and grade spans. In exploring this variation, we defined PPI effects with reference to schools that received a newly placed principal in SY 2012–2013 or later. These analyses for subgroups had weaker statistical power than the overall analysis of PPI effects because of the smaller numbers, but they were consistent with the overall story and lend further support for the inference that the PPI was a benefit to districts.

The PPI effects on reading achievement were positive and statistically significant in five of six districts, and the effects on mathematics achievement were positive and statistically significant in three districts. In one district, the PPI effect on mathematics achievement was negative and statistically significant. In that district, the negative results were concentrated in elementary schools. The three districts that had less of the pipeline in place in SY 2010–2011—and hence the most room to grow during implementation—had positive, statistically significant PPI effects. Retention effects by district were more varied. This variation could reflect differences in the depth of the candidate pool, local factors influencing the labor market for principals, or district approaches to principal reassignment at the start of the initiative.

We found statistically significant positive PPI effects on mathematics achievement for elementary, middle, and high schools and on reading for elementary and middle schools. The broad span of positive effects across these school types is encouraging in view of the challenges that many districts face with staffing administrative positions in middle and high schools.

PPI Effects Kicked in Early

We analyzed effects by cohort, defined in terms of the school year in which new principals were placed. Findings from these analyses suggest that the PPI benefits kicked in quickly: They were evident for the earliest cohorts of PPI principals. Effects on achievement appear to be stable over time for newly placed principals, and the effects on principal retention appear to increase over time.

This is consistent with the general pattern of PPI implementation, year by year. These districts had prior efforts related to the pipeline activities and thus had many of the features in place prior to the launch of the initiative. They made early investments in induction support for novice principals. They then expanded that support while beefing up hiring processes. Moreover, the growth in retention effects over time could indicate that efforts to improve preservice preparation have begun to enhance the quality of the candidate pool or that district efforts in hiring and placement or on-the-job support are improving over time.

Effects of the PPI on Achievement Were Larger for Schools in the Lowest Quartile of the Achievement Distribution

We did subgroup analyses to assess whether the findings were consistent across schools based on their baseline achievement level. We found evidence of larger positive effects of the PPI for schools in the lowest quartile of the statewide achievement distribution (prior to the PPI) compared with schools in the second-lowest quartile for both subjects. Positive effects in this lowest quartile were larger than those for the top quartile in reading, and not smaller than any other quartile.

PPI Components Appear to Work as a Cohesive Whole

Our findings suggest that comprehensive efforts to strategically implement pipeline activities across all components and align them with leader standards—which all districts did—are what matter. We investigated the possibility that specific pipeline components were driving the observed effects using exploratory analyses but found no evidence of clear and consistent relationships between specific components and PPI effects.

The Work Is Affordable: Efforts of PPI Districts to Operate and Enhance Their Pipelines Comprised Less Than 0.5 Percent of District Budgets

It cost a PPI district about $42 per pupil per year, or less than 0.5 percent of the district's budget in each school year, to operate and enhance its principal pipeline. For comparison, the resources that these districts devoted to the PPI are roughly one-quarter of the resources districts in the Intensive Partnerships for Effective Teaching initiative devoted to that work (Stecher et al., 2018, pp. 344–345).

Supporting an initiative such as the PPI involves a broad-based commitment on the part of a school district to have district staff dedicate their time to this work. Nearly half of the PPI expenditures (44 percent) were due to costs of district personnel time devoted to the initiative.

Some of the pipeline work done by districts during the PPI, and accounted for by these cost figures, was devoted to functions that they would have been carrying out anyway, such as hiring, evaluation, and support. We estimated that pipeline expenditures by PPI districts in the year before the launch of the initiative (SY 2010–2011) were at least half (and possibly more) of what they were in the first year of the initiative. The commitment was not just to doing new things but to doing routine things in new ways.

We found that the initiative is quite cost-effective when it comes to raising student achievement. We estimated that for every $100 spent per student attending the district over five years on PPI-related reforms, district-wide student achievement increased by between 1 and 2.4 percentile points in reading and about one-third of a percentile point to 1 percentile point in mathematics. Studies that include both cost estimates and comparable outcome measures for students are not yet common in K–12 education research. Where available, they tend to focus on more-targeted interventions implemented (and paid for) in a shorter time span. Nevertheless, the comparisons we found suggest that, over a five-year period, PPI provided districts with larger gains for fewer resources spent per student than is typically found in research.

Limitations

Features of the PPI and its implementation made it difficult to design a study to definitively measure the initiative's effects. While our findings are robust to a number of sensitivity checks and alternative modeling approaches, we acknowledge important limitations in our ability to attribute effects to the PPI. The districts that were selected for the PPI were chosen in part because they had already implemented some of the pipeline activities prior to initiative. Our approach does not capture effects stemming from district pipeline efforts that might have existed before the initiative began. In implementing pipeline activities, PPI districts continued to modify their approach to activities throughout the initiative. To estimate the effects of the PPI, we compared the changes in outcomes in schools in PPI districts with newly placed principals with the changes in outcomes in similar non-PPI district schools that also received a new principal. We assumed that, absent the PPI, outcomes of schools in PPI districts would have followed a similar trajectory to those of similar schools in non-PPI districts.

Our approach considered the PPI as a district-wide initiative implemented at a specific point in time. It is possible that the effects we have identified are due to other concurrent initiatives or factors that led schools in PPI districts to outperform similar schools in other districts within their state.

Conclusions

Districts matter in shaping school leadership. The work they do to manage principals—through pipeline activities—is important. Our study provides compelling evidence that if districts approach these pipeline activities strategically, paying attention to each component and the coherence of the efforts, they set up their newly placed principals for success. Student achievement outcomes are better, and newly placed principals are more likely to stay in their jobs.

Achievement effects were prevalent across districts, time, and school levels, and stronger effects were observed in schools that received newly placed principals. This provides persuasive evidence that principal pipelines, rather than a set of other disparate factors, were behind the effects we observed. We are aware of no other factor that these districts had in common that would have likely contributed to the effects we measured in this timeframe.

It is feasible to do this work: It happened in six large urban districts that made progress to improve the way they were doing the pipeline activities. It doesn't cost a lot, either.

Districts looking for ways to enhance school outcomes and improve the retention of newly placed principals should be encouraged by the experiences of PPI districts. Our findings suggest that when districts focused attention on activities related to principal pipelines, then principals, schools, and students benefited. There is no single "recipe" for other districts to follow; the initiative looked different on the ground in different districts. In all PPI districts, the work involved analyzing conditions, opportunities, and constraints and making strategic choices based on that assessment. This work involves enduring commitment and an openness to changes in district systems and routines for managing the principalship.

Acknowledgments

This report draws on multiple sources of data about six school districts that participated in The Wallace Foundation's Principal Pipeline Initiative (PPI), as well as data about the states in which those districts are located. The authors are indebted to many people who contributed to the research in a variety of ways.

Above all, we would like to thank staff members in the participating districts who provided us with district-level data on student achievement, school outcomes, school leaders, and resources and expenditures. This research benefited immensely from feedback from superintendents of the participating districts throughout the study. Other district staff provided input into the study design, responded to many rounds of data collection requests over the course of this project, answered our questions about the data, and validated our coding of the cost data. This study would not have been possible without their input. We are especially grateful to the individuals who served as PPI project directors in each district: Jevelyn Bonner-Reed and Rashidah Lopez Morgan of Charlotte-Mecklenburg Schools, Mikel Royal and John Youngquist of Denver Public Schools, Glenn Pethel of Gwinnett County Public Schools, Tricia McManus of Hillsborough County Public Schools, Marina Cofield and Anthony Conelli of the New York City Department of Education, and Doug Anthony and Damaries Blondonville of Prince George's County Public Schools. They provided extensive input and support throughout the project and helped us navigate district requirements related to data requests.

We are indebted to Brenda J. Turnbull of Policy Studies Associates (PSA) for her leadership of this project, her collaboration on the description of implementation findings, her input into the design of this effects study, and her input on multiple draft versions of this report. We also appreciate the collaboration and support we received from Derek Riley, Dan Aladjem, Leslie Anderson, Erikson Arcaira, and Jaclyn MacFarlane of PSA throughout this study. PSA gathered data through surveys administered to principals and assistant principals, as well as interviews conducted with district staff, as part of its evaluation of the implementation of the PPI. Those data and the insights of the PSA research team contributed to our characterization of pipeline implementation. We would also like to thank the senior staff from participating districts who participated in interviews and the principals and assistant principals who participated in surveys.

Mirka Vuollo provided critical support throughout the project, managing the complex research approval and data sharing agreements needed for this project, monitoring timelines, and keeping the work on track.

Numerous current and former RAND colleagues provided feedback on the methods. Isaac Opper reviewed the analytical code. Paul Youngmin Yoo cleaned and analyzed some of the cost data for this study. Yan Wang, Brian Philips, and Alyssa Ramos cleaned and analyzed data for this study. Lucrecia Santibañez participated in the initial evaluation design.

A technical advisory group convened by The Wallace Foundation provided formative feedback on the analytical approach at the project inception and over time. The authors are grateful for the feedback provided by these technical advisors on the methods: Ellen Goldring, Susanna Loeb, Richard Murnane, Jonah Rockoff, and Jesse Rothstein.

We would also like to thank our contacts at The Wallace Foundation who provided substantial input into the design of this study and the communication of findings. In particular, we have benefited from feedback from Elizabeth Ty Wilde, Will Miller, Jody Spiro, Aiesha Eleusizov, Nicholas Pelzer, Rochelle Herring, Edward Pauly, Lucas Bernays Held, Pamela Mendels, and Jessica Schwartz. Kata Mihaly of RAND and Matthew Kraft of Brown University provided helpful reviews of a prior draft of this report, and Lynn Karoly of RAND reviewed the sections on the return on investment. Fatih Unlu managed the peer review process for this report and provided helpful substantive feedback on an earlier draft. Donna White helped to compile and format the final document and provided administrative support throughout the project.

James Torr carefully edited the manuscript and formatted the figures and text boxes. Sandy Petitjean assisted with figure creation, and Monette Velasco effectively managed the production of the final report.

We take full responsibility for any errors.

Abbreviations

AP	assistant principal
CDE	Colorado Department of Education
CITS	comparative interrupted time series
CMO	charter management organization
CO	Colorado
CRCT	Criterion-Referenced Competency Test
CTE	career and technical education
DID	difference-in-difference
ELSI	Elementary and Secondary Information System
EOCT	end-of-course test
FL	Florida
FLDOE	Florida Department of Education
FRL	free or reduced-price lunch
GA	Georgia
GADOE	Georgia Department of Education
GOSA	Governor's Office of Student Achievement
IRB	Institutional Review Board
IRS	Office of Information and Reporting Services
KIPP	Knowledge Is Power Program
LTS	Leader Tracking System
MD	Maryland

MSDE	Maryland State Department of Education
NC	North Carolina
NCDPI	North Carolina Department of Public Instruction
NCERDC	North Carolina Education Data Center
NCES	National Center for Education Statistics
NY	New York
NYSED	New York State Education Department
PD	professional development
PERA	Office of Accountability and Policy Research
PPI	Principal Pipeline Initiative
PSA	Policy Studies Associates
ROI	return on investment
SAM	School Administration Manager
SBE	North Carolina State Board of Education
SY	school year
WWC	What Works Clearinghouse

CHAPTER ONE

Introduction[1]

Districts are a key lever for influencing the quality of school leadership. School districts hire school leaders, give them the important responsibility of running schools, and then support them in that role. Over a decade of research has confirmed that effective school leadership is associated with better outcomes for students and schools (see Branch, Hanushek, and Rivkin, 2012; Grissom, Kalogrides, and Loeb, 2015; Leithwood et al., 2004). A high-quality school leader influences dozens of teachers and hundreds or thousands of students. It is a pivotal role.

A solid base of research demonstrates a link between initiatives targeting school leaders and positive outcomes for students, schools, teachers, and principals (Herman et al., 2017). This research base includes initiatives involving leader-evaluation systems, principal preparation programs, strategic staff management, professional learning for principals and other school leaders, school leader working conditions, and broader school improvement efforts that have a leadership focus. Leithwood et al. (2004) argued that "efforts to improve [school leader] recruitment, training, evaluation and ongoing development should be considered highly cost-effective approaches to successful school improvement" (p. 14). The research base provides guidance regarding specific leadership interventions that can improve the quality of school leadership but is relatively silent on how to implement these interventions at scale.

This study examined strategic efforts on the part of school districts to improve school leadership district-wide. It explored whether school districts can put in place systematic processes that support the strategic management of school leaders, and what happens when they do.

---

[1] This introduction uses material from Kaufman, Gates, et al. (2017). In particular, Text Boxes 1.1 and 1.2 are edited and reformatted versions of Boxes 1.1 and 1.2 in that report. Text Box 3.1 is a reformatted version of material presented in Table 2.1 of Kaufman, Gates, et al. (2017).

The District Role in Improving School Leadership

School districts have wide-ranging responsibilities related to their ultimate objective of educating students. Districts bring a range of resources to bear in pursuit of that objective. The people working for school districts—including teachers and administrators—are an essential resource and effective management of that talent may be critical to student success (Lawler, 2008).

Most public-school principals are employees of districts or charter management organizations (CMOs). The district's effectiveness in defining expectations for and managing school leaders will, in turn, influence the effectiveness of those school leaders. Although principals are often described as the chief executive officers of their schools (Haberman, 2011), in truth, principals working in a district with several, dozens, or hundreds of schools are more like line managers in corporations (see Huselid, Becker, and Beatty, 2005, p. 188). To be sure, principals manage and oversee school-level staff and resources. But they are also responsible for executing the district strategy through use of resources provided to the school by the district. Principals report to and receive support from district-level managers. The district creates the job description and hires principals. These job descriptions establish expectations about what the principal should do in a particular district. District expectations vary, in part, because of district decisions regarding the level of direct support they provide to schools.

Districts, then, are responsible for managing school principals. We use the term *manage* to describe a range of talent management activities, including preservice preparation, hiring, evaluation, professional development (PD), and on-the-job support. All districts devote at least some time and effort to at least some of these talent management activities.

But what happens when districts execute the key talent management functions related to school leadership in a coherent and strategic way? That is what the Principal Pipeline Initiative (PPI) sought to explore.

The Principal Pipeline Initiative

After more than a decade of work on school leadership and the surrounding structures that support it, The Wallace Foundation concluded that principal pipelines could serve as a strategic lever for districts to promote school improvement.[2] The foundation posited that a comprehensive principal pipeline would be more effective than business-as-usual approaches to the preparation and management of school leaders, and it launched the PPI in the summer of 2011 to test that hypothesis in six districts:

---

[2]   For more background on the initiative, see Turnbull, Riley, Arcaira, et al. (2013).

- Charlotte-Mecklenburg Schools, North Carolina
- Denver Public Schools, Colorado
- Gwinnett County Public Schools, Georgia
- Hillsborough County Public Schools, Florida
- New York City Department of Education, New York
- Prince George's County Public Schools, Maryland.

Text Box 1.1 provides an overview of the initiative.

Principal pipeline activities are undertaken by a *district* and its partners to prepare, support, manage, and oversee the work of school leaders in order to ensure their effectiveness (Korach and Cosner, 2017). Principal pipelines comprise four key components: (1) leader standards that guide all pipeline activities, (2) preservice preparation opportunities for assistant principals (APs) and principals (including not only the preservice training itself but also recruitment and selection into these opportunities), (3) selective hiring and placement, and (4) on-the-job induction, evaluation, and support. In addition, the pipeline must develop the capacity, culture, and infrastructure to sustain the work across components. Principal pipeline activities include activities that are referred to as principal talent management or human capital management (George W. Bush Institute, 2016). Any district that employs more than a few principals devotes resources to at least some principal pipeline activities, even if it does not have in place a comprehensive pipeline as defined by the initiative.

As described in Text Box 1.1, the PPI supported strategic improvements to pipeline activities. In particular, leader standards provided the foundation for reforms to other pipeline activities.[3] The six participating districts had already demonstrated a commitment to improving school leadership and had taken some steps toward implementing the components associated with the initiative. They were selected from among a group of 22 urban districts that had "a record of including leadership in their school reform agendas" (The Wallace Foundation, 2011, p. 7) and were invited to apply for the initiative. The selection process considered the capacity of districts to implement the desired approaches in each of the four pipeline components (see Turnbull, Riley, Arcaira, et al., 2013). The initiative was about ensuring a comprehensive and strategic approach to a set of activities rather than adopting prespecified changes to any one activity or set of activities.

---

[3]   Grissom, Blissett, and Mitani (2018) describe the challenges in identifying the standards that can serve as a basis for principal evaluation.

Text Box 1.1. The Principal Pipeline Initiative

The PPI provided resources to six urban school districts to put in place a pipeline for preparing and supporting novice principals. Each district was expected to align preservice preparation, selective hiring and placement, and evaluation and support with leadership standards. Districts were also expected to develop systems of support to sustain these efforts after the end of the grant period. The Wallace Foundation selected six districts that already viewed school leadership as an important lever for school improvement and that were already using the principal pipeline as a strategic lever for school improvement. The foundation provided resources to these districts in order to catalyze those efforts and develop principal pipelines as defined by the grant.

To support this work, The Wallace Foundation initially awarded each district $7.5 million to $12.5 million (see Wallace Foundation, 2011). The foundation supplemented that initial funding with targeted technical assistance to support structured interactions with preservice preparation providers through Quality Measures (a tool that the Education Development Center developed for improving partnerships between school districts and principal preservice preparation providers), the development of leader tracking systems (LTSs), and additional funding of $430,000 to $1 million per district to improve principal supervision (Wallace Foundation, 2014). Districts also leveraged funding from federal sources (e.g., Titles I and II of the Elementary and Secondary Education Act, Race to the Top), state and local sources, and support from foundations to support initiative activities. A series of implementation reports by Policy Studies Associates (PSA), culminating in Turnbull, Anderson, et al. (2016), documented the starting point for each district, as well as the changes each district undertook.[a]

These reports indicated that districts varied in terms of their starting points with respect to each initiative component, as well as areas of intended focus for the initiative. At the same time, each district was able to implement and sustain enhancements to its pipeline and institutionalize features of principal pipelines that research has indicated are critical to success. Notably, each district did the following:

- developed or revised leader standards and utilized those standards to align and guide preservice preparation, selective hiring, and on-the-job evaluation and support
- developed partnerships with principal preservice providers and/or developed or refined in-house principal preparation programs
- revised principal hiring and placement processes to be informed by more data and aligned with leader standards
- revised principal-evaluation processes to align with leader standards and inform development and delivery of on-the-job support
- developed LTSs (see Text Box 1.2).

While not a requirement of the PPI, five of the six districts reduced the number of principals that each principal supervisor oversees—or the "span of control"—and reshaped the job of principal supervisors. The districts also worked to improve the quality of preservice preparation options, developing or improving their own preservice preparation programs and/or promoting improvement in programs with university or nonprofit partners. Recognizing that these preservice preparation program improvement efforts take several years or more to improve the quality of sitting principals, districts participating in the PPI prioritized efforts described in the bulleted list above (Turnbull, Riley, Arcaira, et al., 2013, p. 36). Participating districts pursued and continue to pursue their pipeline enhancement work using a continuous quality improvement approach—starting small and learning from preliminary implementation to make adjustments while moving forward (see Turnbull, Anderson, et al., 2016).

[a] See Wallace Foundation (undated) for the complete series.

Text Box 1.2. Leader Tracking Systems

Each of the participating districts developed a Leader Tracking System (LTS): a database with longitudinal information about current and aspiring principals that would potentially support data-driven decisionmaking regarding principal selection, hiring, and support, as well as meet the data requirements of a rigorous evaluation of the initiative. Developing an LTS required each district to identify all the relevant data sources regarding current and aspiring principals (typically housed in different offices across the district); address issues with data quality, including critical gaps in the data; compile the data into a usable, longitudinal format; and develop user-friendly systems through which district personnel could access information that would meet their most-pressing needs (Anderson, Turnbull, and Arcaira, 2017).

To accomplish this work, each district "established cross-departmental teams" (Gill, 2016, p. 3) that included representatives from several different departments, such as human resources, leadership development, talent management, information technology, business applications, and business systems. Several districts also hired outside consultants to assist with the initial information technology systems and database software development while training in-house staff to manage the work in the future. In addition, The Wallace Foundation funded a technical assistance provider to provide guidance on LTS development in each district.

The resulting LTS in each district contained information on current and aspiring principals' educational background, employment history within and outside the district, ratings by teachers, ratings by supervisors, specialized skills of interest to the district, and test scores of students at current and previous schools, as well as other information. The vast majority of district officials in all participating districts indicated that they found the LTS to be worthwhile or very worthwhile, according to an informal survey conducted by The Wallace Foundation (Gill, 2016).

Principal Pipeline Activities Hold Potential to Improve School Leadership and Reduce Turnover

All pipeline activities, if done well, have potential to improve the quality of the people leading schools and, in particular, the quality of those newly hired into leadership positions. They represent an investment in better leaders and, in turn, better teachers and better and more-equitable outcomes for kids (Curtis and Wurtzel, 2010). Grissom and Bartanen (2018) found that high-performing principals—those who are rated highly by their supervisors and whose schools experience high achievement growth—have lower turnover than low-performing principals. Principal turnover is both costly and disruptive to schools and districts. Evidence suggests that it can cost $75,000 for a district to replace a principal (School Leaders Network, 2014). Other sectors view leadership as an investment, as well.

The notion that quality leadership can benefit organizations is not unique to public education. A 2016 survey of more than 7,000 businesses and human resources

(HR) leaders in more than 130 countries found that leadership is a high-priority issue across countries and sectors (Wakefield et al., 2016, p. 27). Corporate spending on leadership has been on the increase and studies suggest that high-performing companies spend as much as four times more than their competitors on leadership (Wakefield et al., 2016, p. 28). In addition to better organizational outcomes, the HR management literature suggests that efforts similar to those included in the PPI can reduce employee turnover (Allen, Bryant, and Vardaman, 2010). By reducing turnover, school districts can avoid turnover costs. The HR literature suggests that turnover costs can be substantial—ranging from 75 to 200 percent of salary costs (Cascio, 2006). Lower turnover could also have implications for future spending on the principal pipeline, although it is beyond the scope of our study to capture those effects. Having fewer leadership vacancies because of turnover could lead to reduced district spending on preparation, hiring, and early-career support over time.

This Report Documents Implementation and Effects of the PPI

Our objectives for this study were fourfold:

1. Describe what policies, procedures, and practices six urban districts were able to change when implementing principal pipelines and how they affected pipeline participants.
2. Characterize the effect of the PPI on student outcomes, principal retention, and other outcomes, including school climate, stakeholder satisfaction, and teacher turnover, and to understand whether and how those effects varied by district, cohort, principal, and school characteristics.
3. Explore the mechanisms through which effects are realized.
4. Relate these findings to previously collected information regarding the costs of implementing principal pipelines (Kaufman, Gates, et al., 2017).

We map these objectives to the following four research questions:

- What policies, procedures, and practices were districts able to change when implementing principal pipelines, and how did they affect pipeline participants?
- What was the overall effect of principal pipelines on key school-level outcomes, and how do the effects of principal pipelines vary by district, cohort, and school characteristics?
- Which components of principal pipelines are related to effects?
- Are principal pipelines cost-effective? Which pipeline components appear to be most cost-effective?

This is the first evaluation report about the PPI to present information on pipe-line effects from sources other than surveys of new principals. It complements the evaluation study's five implementation reports, based on interview and survey data, that documented what PPI districts did to build a pipeline with the key components and operate that pipeline at scale.[4] These five reports describe how the PPI districts did the work of building a pipeline and, in detail, what implementation in each district looked like as of 2015. A sixth report, on LTSs, describes what an LTS is and how PPI districts used it to support their pipeline efforts (Anderson, Turnbull, and Arcaira, 2017). A seventh report, on resources and expenditure, describes what resources are needed to build and support a principal pipeline (Kaufman, Gates, et al., 2017). An eighth report, on sustainability, describes what can be sustained over the long term and how districts can ensure sustainability of these efforts (Anderson and Turnbull, 2019)

Scope of the PPI

The PPI was implemented by districts that had already taken steps to strategically improve the way they manage school leaders. Our study findings are most relevant to districts operating in similar contexts to the six large urban public-school districts that participated in the PPI. Each of the PPI districts

- was among the 50 largest school districts in the United States
- served more than 80,000 students and operated more than 130 schools
- was a "minority-majority" district, serving a student population that was some-where between 65 percent and 96 percent minority depending on the district and school year
- had demonstrated a commitment to school leadership improvement and had undertaken some efforts related to principal pipelines prior to the launch of the initiative.

While the lessons we derived from this study are most readily generalizable to other large districts that view school leadership as a strategic lever for school reform and have the capacity to implement pipeline components, the findings may also be of interest to any organization that has to make strategic choices about how it prepares, manages, and supports school leaders. This includes

---

[4]   These reports are Turnbull, Riley, Arcaira, et al. (2013); Turnbull, Riley, and MacFarlane (2013); Turnbull, Riley, and MacFarlane (2015); Anderson and Turnbull (2016); and Turnbull, Anderson, et al., (2016). They are all available for download at http://www.wallacefoundation.org/knowledge-center/pages/building-a-stronger-principalship.aspx.

- districts that have not yet made a commitment to school leadership as a lever to promote school improvement
- districts that are smaller than the PPI districts but still play a role in managing school leaders—on their own or in collaboration with other districts
- CMOs that manage a cadre of school leaders.
- state education agencies, principal preparation programs, and policymakers in other organizations.

Other districts that seek to apply lessons from this evaluation must bear in mind that they may be embarking on such efforts from a different starting point. This could imply the need for more investments and more time to go by before the payoffs are realized.

The initiative involved improvements to activities for which districts are responsible with or without an initiative like the PPI. The initiative asked districts to undertake comprehensive efforts to align the activities to district standards for school leaders, but the PPI left districts with a substantial amount of flexibility regarding what they emphasized and when in the course of the five-year initiative. This implies that the initiative looked different on the ground in different districts. It also implies that there is no "recipe" for other districts to follow. The work involved analyzing conditions, opportunities, and constraints and making strategic choices based on that assessment.

Caveats

The design of the PPI posed challenges for evaluating its effects. In order to estimate causal effects of the initiative, we had to grapple with the following questions:

- What schools are affected—or *treated*—by the PPI?
- When would effects be observable?
- What would we expect performance to look like in the absence of the PPI?

We describe how we resolved these questions and the implications for our approach.

What Schools Are Treated by the PPI?
The PPI focused on novice principals and we expected that the schools most affected by the initiative would be those that get a newly placed principal after the implementation of the PPI. However, many of the pipeline activities (especially standards, evaluation, supervision, and support) could benefit other schools as well. Our primary analysis of the PPI effects focused on newly placed principals and the schools they lead, but we also examined whether the PPI had an effect on all schools in the district.

When Would We Expect to See an Effect of the PPI?

Because the PPI represented a set of guidelines rather than a specific recipe, PPI districts did different things at different times. As described above, districts were selected for the PPI because they already had some of the features in place. Even when districts had a component in place, they continued to modify their pipeline activities throughout the initiative and beyond. That made it difficult to identify a point in time when the PPI was "implemented" in every district. Ultimately, we decided to consider schools to be treated in school year (SY) 2012–2013 or later—when key elements of the pipeline had been at least partially implemented by all districts. We acknowledge that treatment might have kicked in earlier, in which case our analysis would be underestimating the effects of the PPI.

What Would We Expect Performance to Look Like in the Absence of the PPI?

We assumed that, in the absence of the PPI, the change in outcomes over time in PPI-treated schools would follow the same trajectory as the change in outcomes for similar schools in non-PPI districts in the same state. Standard approaches to validating this assumption are less useful than is often the case in program evaluation given the nature of this initiative. Notably, because PPI districts were selected for participation because they were already in the process of implementing pipeline activities, it is quite possible that outcomes were already improving relative to other districts in the state prior to SY 2012–2013. To the extent that this is true, our approach captures the combined effect of the selection of PPI districts and their implementation of the PPI itself. We nevertheless undertook a number of standard specification checks. These involved running different versions of the model and comparing the results we got using different approaches. We found that our results were robust to these alternative approaches.

Limitations

The caveats described in the preceding section imply important limitations in our ability to definitively measure the initiative's effects and to attribute the effects we measure to the PPI.

Because our approach considered the PPI as a district-wide initiative implemented at a specific point in time, it is possible that the effects we identified are due to other concurrent initiatives or factors that led schools in PPI districts to perform differently than similar schools in other districts within their state.

There are no systematic studies documenting "business as usual" with regard to district involvement in the full range of pipeline activities during the timeframe of this evaluation, nor do we have data on what other districts in the same state as PPI districts were doing in the area. The premise of the PPI was that while some school districts are thinking about school leadership and undertaking initiatives related to specific components of the pipeline, few or no districts were taking a strategic approach to the full range of pipeline activities. We approached this analysis from the perspective that other districts in each state were engaged in at least some pipeline activities and may have had specific initiatives related to specific activities but that they were not addressing all four pipeline components in a strategic way.

Confidentiality about district-specific results was a requirement of the study. Therefore, we present district-specific results in a de-identified format, taking care not to associate results in a way that would allow readers to infer results for any district. This limited our ability to highlight associations between implementation and effects findings.

Overview of This Report

In Chapter Two, we describe our research questions in more detail and provide an overview of the data and methods we rely on to answer those questions. Additional details about the data and methods are provided in the appendixes. Chapter Three presents findings related to the implementation of the PPI. We describe district policies, procedures, and practices for the management of school leaders just before the start of the PPI (as of SY 2010–2011), the extent to which pipeline components had been implemented as of SY 2016–2017, and the path between those two points. We also describe ways in which the experiences of school leaders in the PPI districts changed during the initiative. Chapter Four presents findings about the effect of the PPI. We consider the effect of the PPI on student achievement, principal retention, and other school outcomes. We describe the results of our subgroup and sensitivity analyses and discuss the estimated academic return on investment (ROI) from the PPI. Chapter Five discusses the findings and presents recommendations. The appendixes describe the technical details of our data collection and analysis. Appendix A provides additional detail on data sources. Appendix B elaborates on the methods used for analysis. Appendix C describes the matching process used to identify comparison schools. Appendix D provides additional detail on results that are likely to be of interest to technical readers. Appendix E presents additional detail on our analysis of academic ROI.

CHAPTER TWO

Research Approach

This study relied on a range of data sources and qualitative and quantitative analytical methods. In this chapter, we describe the research questions and provide an overview of the data and our analytic approach. We also discuss the scope and limitations of our analysis. More-detailed information about data and methods is provided in Appendixes A–E, as noted throughout the chapter.

Data

The data sources for our study included the following:[1]

- **District data on students, schools, and principals.** Each of the PPI districts provided extensive academic and administrative data about students, schools, and staff. All districts provided these data from at least SY 2010–2011 through SY 2016–2017. Notably, LTS data included records of the characteristics, placements, and pipeline-related experiences of school principals, especially principals who were newly placed during this period.
- **State data on students, schools, and principals.** We assembled and obtained data on students, schools, and principals at the school level from each state that contained a PPI district. This included whether the school had a newly placed principal, principal tenure, student demographic information, student achievement, other student outcomes, school climate ratings, school-level teacher turnover, and teacher certification rates.
- **Data collected for the implementation and cost studies.** PSA administered a survey to all principals who had been in their roles for three years or fewer in 2013, 2014, and 2015. This report uses data collected in 2014 and 2015. The survey asked these novice principals and APs a range of questions about their

---

[1] Data were collected and obtained over the course of the initiative by RAND and PSA. Each organization has an Institutional Review Board (IRB) that reviewed the collection and use of human subjects data. Additionally, the study established data-use agreements with participating states and districts, as required.

experiences in the principal pipeline. More information about the survey is available in Turnbull, Anderson, et al. (2016) and in Appendix A.[2] In addition, PSA and RAND researchers conducted numerous interviews with district personnel who managed or played key roles in the initiative to gather more information about pipeline implementation, resources, and expenditures. For the cost study, RAND researchers developed a separate tool to gather data from districts on all staff involved in principal pipeline activities, the percentage of their time they spent on the pipeline over the course of the year, the specific activities that they performed, and their annual salaries and benefits.

- **District progress reports to Wallace.** Throughout the initiative, districts provided progress reports to The Wallace Foundation. These progress reports provided an overview of what each district had accomplished in the prior year and what it was focusing attention on in the coming year. They also provided information on preferred preservice programs and the number of candidates who had completed or were attending such programs. Finally, progress reports included information on the number of new principal hires and projections of expected principal vacancies.

Overview of Research Approach

To address the research questions described in Chapter One, we used multiple methods. The centerpiece of this study was an analysis of outcomes for schools in PPI districts that received a newly placed principal in SY 2012–2013 or later compared with schools in non-PPI districts that also received a newly placed principal in the same year. We used this analysis to characterize the effect of the PPI overall and for key subgroups of interest. We supplemented this with descriptive and exploratory analyses that provided context for the effects findings, insights into the mechanisms by which the effects might be generated, and insights regarding the academic ROI for the initiative. Table 2.1 summarizes the relationship between these approaches and the research questions. We briefly elaborate on each methodological approach below. Detailed information can be found in the appendixes.

Analysis of Data Gathered from Districts

We analyzed and compiled a wide range of student-, school-, and principal-level data provided to us by PPI districts in order to develop descriptive summaries of how things changed (or did not change) in PPI districts during the timeframe of the initiative.

---

[2]   The response rates for the survey were relatively high in both 2014 and 2015. As reported in Turnbull, Anderson, et al. (2016), the number of novice principals across participating districts who responded to the survey was 541 in 2014 and 514 in 2015, for average response rates of 66 and 65 percent, respectively. The average response rates for districts other than New York City were more than 85 percent in each year.

Table 2.1
Approach Used to Address Research Questions

Research Question	Data and Methods Used
What policies, procedures, and practices were districts able to change when implementing principal pipelines, and how did these changes affect pipeline participants?	Descriptive characterization drawing on LTS, survey, cost study, and implementation study data
What was the overall effect of principal pipelines on key school-level outcomes, and how did these effects vary by district, cohort, and school characteristics?	Regression analysis of outcomes for schools with newly placed principals in PPI districts compared with outcomes for schools with newly placed principals in other districts across the state using state data Regression analysis of outcomes for all schools in PPI districts compared with outcomes for schools in other districts across the state
Which components of principal pipelines are correlated with effects?	Examination of correlations between school-level effects and pipeline exposure
Are principal pipelines cost-effective? Which pipeline components appear to be most cost-effective?	Analysis of the relationship between school-level effects and pipeline cost estimates developed for cost study

The PPI required districts to develop LTSs, which include rich data about current and aspiring school leaders in the district. We were able to associate the data on each principal with the schools they eventually led.

Descriptive Characterization of Implementation

To characterize implementation of the PPI by district, we reviewed findings from prior studies, consulted with the implementation evaluation team at PSA, and analyzed administrative data provided to us by PPI districts as described above.

Outcomes Analysis

A primary objective of this study was to characterize the effects of the PPI in the districts that participated. We did this by comparing principal retention and changes in school outcomes for PPI district schools relative to changes in the same outcomes for similar non-PPI schools, an approach referred to as a difference-in-difference (DID) methodology. The approach is designed to capture the overall effect of the PPI in a school district and sheds light on the question of how much other districts might benefit if they took the same steps as the PPI districts and could access the same supports. The basic intuition is described in Text Box 2.1.

To estimate the primary effect of interest—what we refer to throughout as the *PPI effect*—we focused specifically on schools that got a newly placed principal in SY 2012–2013 or later. Only these schools in PPI districts are considered *treated* in this main analysis. Overall, on average, 56 percent of the schools in PPI districts received a new principal during the period of the study and are included in the primary analysis.

Text Box 2.1. Intuition Behind Our Methodology for Estimating Main PPI Effects

We used a DID approach to estimate the causal effects of the PPI on school outcomes.

- The approach starts by defining a set of schools that are affected—or treated—by the PPI.
- We then compare the change in outcomes for these treated schools with the change in outcomes for a set of similar schools that were not treated by the PPI (comparison schools).
  - Comparison schools are schools in non-PPI districts in the same state.
  - Comparison schools were selected based on their similarity to treated schools in the PPI districts using matching methods described in Appendix C.
- We assume that, in the absence of the PPI, the change in outcomes over time in PPI-treated schools would follow a similar trajectory to the change in outcomes for comparison schools.
- The **PPI effect** is the extent to which the change in outcomes of treated schools is better (or worse) than the change in outcomes in comparison schools.
  - The PPI effect would be **positive** if treated schools in PPI districts have better student achievement outcomes than expected based on the experience of similar schools in non-PPI districts.
  - The PPI effect would be **negative** if treated schools in PPI districts have worse student achievement outcomes than expected based on the experience of similar schools in non-PPI districts.

We did not estimate the performance of individual principals. When analyzing school outcomes, once a school is identified as treated because it received a newly placed principal, we considered the school as treated for as long as the school is present in the data—even if that principal leaves the school. *Positive* PPI effects imply that the changes in the outcomes of the schools that received newly placed principals in PPI districts were *better* than the changes experienced by comparison schools. For example, with respect to achievement, better changes could mean larger gains or smaller losses. *Negative* PPI effects imply that the changes in outcomes for schools that received newly placed principals in PPI districts were *worse* than the changes experienced by comparison schools.

We used statewide data to identify comparison schools in non-PPI districts that were similar to the treated schools—not only in terms of getting a new principal in the same school year, but also being the same school type (elementary or secondary, newly opened or not) and having similar school-level characteristics at baseline with respect to the outcome of interest and student demographics. Only similar comparison schools were included in the analysis. The matching approach we used to identify eligible comparison schools and the process by which it is incorporated into the subsequent analysis are described in detail in Appendix C.

We chose to draw comparisons from across the state, rather than from one or two comparison districts, for two reasons. First, this approach gave us a broader set of schools from which to select matches for the treated schools. Second, this approach supports the robustness of our analysis by limiting the influence of any district-wide initiatives in any one comparison district on our effect estimates.

Having restricted the comparison sample to schools that are well matched to the PPI district schools, we estimated the effect of the PPI at two time points relative to the arrival of a new principal: two years after the principal change and three or more years after that change. We attempted to control for unobserved differences that do not vary over time through a modeling approach that includes fixed effects. We also controlled for several school characteristics, such as student demographics, enrollment, principal experience, and school type (e.g., elementary school, middle school, high school, charter school).

We analyzed effects separately by PPI district. Then, to create an overall estimate of the effect of the PPI, we aggregated those estimates across the six districts by taking the simple average of the by-district effects. This means that our estimate reflects the average effect of the PPI on treated schools (or their students) in the school districts that implemented it. The estimate sheds light on how much another district might benefit if it took the same steps as the PPI districts and could access the same supports. This approach also avoids having the largest PPI district driving the results, as it would under an approach that weighted the results by the number of schools or students that are treated. We calculate the standard error of this average by assuming independence of the treatment effect estimates across districts. These average estimates may be interpreted as the average gain in percentile scores for having a newly placed PPI principal instead of a newly placed non-PPI principal in observationally similar schools, for two years after placement of the new principal, and for three or more years after their placement.

We evaluated two primary outcomes of interest. The first is student achievement (mathematics and reading) based on average student test scores on standardized tests in the state. We standardized tests within grade, year, and subject and then transformed these into percentile points of achievement after estimation for ease of interpretation. The second primary outcome of interest is retention as a principal in the same school. We evaluated retention into the second and third year after being placed. We consider success of the program to be reflected in larger gains (or smaller losses) in student achievement relative to comparison schools and higher rates of principal retention in treated schools relative to comparison schools. Text Box 2.2 describes the reasons for looking at two-year and three-year retention. We additionally consider several other outcomes, where available for each state—including attendance rates, graduation rates, school discipline rates, teacher retention rates, and school climate surveys. More details on these outcomes are contained in Appendix B.

Text Box 2.2. Retention of Newly Placed Principals

We analyzed retention of newly placed principals in the same school as a principal into the second and third year after placement. Retention was a natural outcome to explore in this evaluation because principal turnover is costly for districts and disruptive for schools, teachers, and students. Research has shown that urban school districts and especially schools serving high-needs student populations tend to have higher principal turnover. Nationwide, 18 percent of public school principals in the 2015–2016 school year were no longer serving in the same role in the following school year. Six percent had moved to become principals at another school, and 10 percent had left the principalship. School-level turnover was higher (21 percent) in schools where 75 percent or more of the students are eligible for free and reduced-price lunch. Urban and rural schools have lower annual retention than suburban schools and those located in towns (U.S. Department of Education, 2018a).

Retention metrics can be difficult to interpret because a principal may leave his or her job for many reasons:

- Poorly performing principals may be asked or choose to leave. The logic of the PPI was to improve the quality of the candidate pool and the ability of districts to effectively place those candidates into schools. At the start of the PPI, all six districts felt there was room for improvement with regard to principal preparation and viewed principal hiring as a "pain point" (see Turnbull, Anderson, et al., 2016, p. 25). Lacking systematic data for assessing strength and weaknesses of candidates and matching those to the needs of the schools, most districts engaged in somewhat ad hoc processes. The PPI should have reduced the chances that districts would hire a poorly performing principal.

- Well-performing principals may be promoted to become principal supervisors or moved to a new setting where their skills can be put to better use. Indeed, some PPI district officials said they were reassigning successful principals to high-needs schools, although they hoped that efforts to develop the candidate pool would limit the need to make quick reassignments of new rising stars.

- Well-performing principals may choose to leave their position. We expect that if the PPI improved working conditions and support for principals, they would be less inclined to leave voluntarily.

In view of research showing that the actions taken by principals to affect student achievement take time to implement and pay off (Coelli and Green, 2012; Rangel, 2018), we approached this analysis from the perspective that if a principal is performing well and the district has an adequate pipeline of staff to fill important roles, the district would prefer to leave a newly placed principal in place for at least two and ideally three years.

In estimating effects for newly placed principals, we combined information for multiple cohorts of newly placed principals—those placed as principals in SY 2012–2013 through SY 2014–2015 for the estimates of effects over three or more years, and those placed in SY 2012–2013 through SY 2015–2016 for the estimates of effects over two years.

Although we expected that the PPI would primarily affect newly placed principals, we also considered whether the PPI had a district-wide effect on achievement outcomes in all schools, as described in Text Box 2.3. The analysis of district-wide effects included all schools that were in the district as of SY 2012–2013—not only those that received a newly placed principal. We examined outcomes two years and three or more years after SY 2012–2013. When presenting estimates of the district-wide effects, we use the same methods to present the effect for the subsample of schools that received a newly placed principal in SY 2012–2013.

Text Box 2.3. District-Wide Effects of the PPI

In addition to our main analysis focused on schools that get a newly placed principal, we also considered whether there is an effect of the PPI on all schools in the district. As described in the introduction, it is possible that the PPI affected all schools in the district—not just those that receive a new principal. For instance, reforms to district-wide systems such as professional standards and evaluation systems could improve the performance of all principals, and changes in principal hiring practices could influence the composition of veteran district principals (for example, by reducing the number of poorly performing principals remaining on the job). Therefore, we estimated treatment effects for all schools in PPI districts. For this analysis, we also broadened the comparison group beyond schools in non-PPI districts across the state that received a newly placed principal. In this specification, we considered SY 2012–2013 as the first year of treatment for all schools in the PPI districts, with SY 2013–2014 the second year and all subsequent years the third and later years. We contrasted the results from this alternative specification with findings for the 2013 cohort analysis of the primary model to compare whether the effects are different for newly placed principals than for all principals.

Subgroup Analysis

We also estimated PPI effects for different subgroups of schools that get newly placed principals. The analytic approach was the same as the approach to estimating main effects but applied to specific subgroups of schools. Below, we describe the types of subgroup analysis we conducted and what we hoped to learn from each analysis:

- Grade level: We analyzed outcomes separately for elementary, middle, and high schools to see whether PPI effects vary by school type. This analysis shed light on, for example, how elementary schools that get a newly placed principal in PPI districts are doing relative to comparison elementary schools.

- District: To the extent that effects have a similar direction across the six districts, there is additional support for the hypothesis that the PPI, rather than something else, is behind an overall finding.
- Cohorts: We estimated effects of the PPI for cohorts of newly placed principals defined by the school year in which they were placed. If the PPI reforms took time to affect principals' experiences, we might not see any effect for early PPI cohorts. If the PPI reforms kicked in quickly, we would expect to see the effect for those principals who were newly placed in SY 2012–2013.
- New to district hires versus reassigned principals: The PPI was designed primarily with novice principals in mind, and many of the activities—such as enhancements to preservice, revisions to hiring practices and induction support for novice principals—applied primarily to this group. However, data limitations at the state level prevented us from doing a rigorous comparative analysis of novice principals, because we cannot distinguish among novice principals, new to district hires, and reassigned principals in the state data (see Text Box 2.4 for definitions of these terms). Since we could partially distinguish among these groups for the PPI districts, we examined whether the effects are larger or smaller for new principal hires versus reassigned principals. We would expect to see larger effects for new principal hires.[3]
- We analyzed whether PPI effects vary based on criteria commonly used to identify high-needs schools. Our main subgroup analysis in this vein considered subgroups created based on the quartile of achievement in the baseline year using the statewide data. We also analyzed outcomes for subgroups of schools serving more than 50 percent and more than 75 percent non-white students and those serving more than 50 percent and more than 75 percent students eligible for free or reduced-price lunch. Appendix D explains the reasons for these thresholds, and Figure D.10 describes how treated schools are distributed across the baseline achievement quartiles.

Additionally, we analyzed subgroups of subgroups in some cases to better understand patterns that were emerging in the subgroup analysis. For example, to understand patterns by cohort, we looked at patterns by cohort for new principal hires and reassigned principals.

---

[3]   This subgroup analysis has additional limitations. Because we can distinguish between new district hires and reassigned principals only for the PPI districts, our subgroup analysis is comparing outcomes for new district hires in PPI districts with all newly placed principals in non-PPI districts. Since we cannot always control for principal tenure because of data limitations, we are at times comparing a novice PPI principal with non-PPI principals who may have substantial principal experience. To the extent that experienced principals have better outcomes, this could bias our estimate of effects for new principal hires downward, because outcomes for those schools are being compared with those of more experienced principals in those districts.

Text Box 2.4. Types of Newly Placed Principals

Newly placed principals are defined as principals who assume the principalship in a school for the first time in a given school year. The group of newly placed principals includes:

- **Reassigned principals:** individuals who have experience as a principal in another school in the same district.

- **New principal hires:** Individuals who are serving as a principal in the district for the first time.

New principal hires can include:

- **Novice principals:** Individuals with no prior experience as a principal. These individuals may have been working in the district as a teacher, assistant principal, or other administrator, or be hired from outside the district.

- **Experienced out-of-district hires:** Individuals who previously served as a principal in another district or a charter school.

District and state data limit the ability of analysts and district managers to distinguish among these groups. Typically, state (or district) data systems do not track the total amount of experience a person has as a principal in a state (or district). In view of research showing that the actions taken by principals to affect student achievement take time to implement and pay off (Coelli and Green, 2012; Rangel, 2018), we approached this analysis from the perspective that if a principal is preforming well and the district has an adequate pipeline of staff to fill important roles, the district would prefer to leave a newly placed principal in place for at least two and ideally three years.

Effect estimates for a particular subgroup reflect how much treated schools in that subgroup are outperforming or underperforming comparison schools that also belong to that subgroup. They do not imply that one subgroup had better outcomes than another in absolute terms (for example, that treated elementary schools ended up with better achievement results than treated middle schools).

The subgroup analyses were as rigorous as the main analysis, but because they involve smaller samples, they had less power to detect statistically significant effects. In describing the subgroup findings, we explicitly note when effects estimates are significant—meaning that the change in outcomes between treated and comparison schools for that subgroup is different from zero and statistically significant.[4]

---

[4]   We did not correct standard errors for multiple hypotheses, so some of the statistically significant findings could be due to random chance. In reporting statistically significant findings, we highlight those for which the level of confidence about the significance is 95 percent. That means there is a 5 percent chance that any one finding is actually not different from zero. Examining several different subgroups increased the chances that we might, by chance, get a "false positive" finding in one or more subgroups.

For some of the subgroup analyses, there were minor limitations with the potential to introduce bias or influence interpretation. We highlight those limitations in Chapter Four. In general, we were interested in the relative size of PPI effects and whether the direction of the PPI effects we measured was the same across subgroups.

Sensitivity Checks

Sensitivity checks allowed us to explore how sensitive our results are to key assumptions in the main analytical approach. The sensitivity analyses on our empirical model are described in Chapter Four and the appendixes. We also performed an analysis that includes charter schools for all districts and the noncharter schools, even for PPI districts that do not have jurisdiction over the charter schools. This sensitivity check aims to gauge whether our findings are meaningfully influenced by independently managed schools that may have been less directly affected by the PPI reforms.

Finally, we evaluated how sensitive the results are to the inclusion of newly opened schools by dropping these schools from the analysis. This sensitivity check assesses the extent to which our findings are dependent on schools for which we lack a lengthy historical record of performance that we can control for in our models.

Exploratory Analyses

Having examined the effects of the PPI overall and for different subgroups, we conducted two types of exploratory analyses to examine the relationship between PPI and other outcomes and the relationship between PPI effects and the implementation of specific PPI components. Because of data limitations and the nature of PPI implementation, these analyses have limitations that distinguish them from the main and subgroup analyses described above. Findings from these analyses would provide insights into but not conclusive evidence about the underlying relationships.

First, we were interested in exploratory analysis regarding the impact of the intervention on additional student and teacher outcomes. We performed this analysis using the same empirical methodology described above as related to student achievement and principal retention, but we consider it to be exploratory in nature because we did not have common outcome measures for all districts. Findings related to these other outcomes are based on data for the districts that had data available on each outcome, which was from one to four districts depending on the outcome.

Second, we explored whether effects vary by a school's exposure to different pipeline components (leader standards, preservice reforms, selective hiring processes, evaluation systems, and professional development and other supports) as well as whether they vary based on a range of school characteristics. We examined these questions through a noncausal, exploratory analysis in which we essentially created an effect measure for each treated school using a version of the main analytical approach described above. Then we performed a regression analysis to understand relationships between these effect measures and indicators of pipeline exposure for that school. The results can provide clues about how the PPI played out but should be interpreted with caution.

A key challenge we faced in trying to disentangle the effects of different pipeline components is that there is no clear way to isolate and directly measure the separate contribution of each PPI component. PPI-related reforms were implemented in tandem and strategically, with potential for significant inter-dependency and selection biases in any resulting impacts. In addition, the fact that districts selected for the PPI had already made progress on some of the components further limits our ability to detect the benefits of those components. Finally, even when we can observe the implementation of a component during the study period, there could be a delay between implementation and effects. Such lagging effects might not be observed or clearly distinguished from the effects of components that were implemented later. Still, we employed a mix of exploratory analysis methods, described fully in Appendix B, that seek to provide partial insights into how these components might have contributed to the overall PPI effects.

These analyses provided clues about how the PPI played out but, given their exploratory nature, should be interpreted with caution.

Analysis of Return on Investment

We used our estimates of the PPI's impacts on achievement outcomes (as described above), in combination with comprehensive cost data collected from five of the six PPI districts as part of the resources and expenditure study (Kaufman, Gates, et al., 2017) to develop an approximate measure of academic ROI from pipeline activities. In doing so, we focused on just the period in which the PPI was implemented, for which we have both cost data and effect estimates.[5] Our academic ROI is thus (conservatively) based on the effects of five years of investment in PPI-related reforms and on whatever effects we observe in those five years, without assuming any lingering or downstream effects of the PPI-related spending over that period. Academic ROI is calculated as the ratio of these dollars spent per student to the average academic effect sizes that students in schools with new principals experienced.

In this report, we did not translate the estimated *academic* ROI into a measure of *economic* ROI in students' long-term life outcomes; doing so would require a variety of assumptions that are outside of the scope of our report. Nevertheless, our measure of academic ROI provides a useful comparison point regarding the cost-effectiveness of PPI reforms relative to that of other educational interventions that influence students' academic performance. It could also be described as an analysis of the *cost-*

---

[5]   Specifically, we use our complete cost data from the period from SY 2011–2012 through SY 2014–2015 to estimate an average per-student cost per year, and then assume costs were comparable through the fifth year of the study, SY 2015–2016.

effectiveness of the intervention. (See Text Box 2.5 for a summary of the terminology used to describe analyses of education interventions.)

We considered academic ROI for the primary effects specific to students in schools led by newly placed principals over the period of the study, and we considered academic ROI using estimates of the district-wide effects of the PPI. In brief, our academic ROI estimates used the estimated effects of the PPI and related that to the estimated per-student costs of the PPI from the 2017 cost study analysis. The details of our academic ROI calculation are provided in Appendix E.

Our estimate for the academic ROI of the PPI has some important limitations. First, it is dependent on the accuracy of our estimation of the causal effects of the

---

Text Box 2.5. Types of Economic Evidence About Education Interventions

As described in a 2016 report by the National Academies of Sciences, Engineering, and Medicine, there are many different ways of looking at cost or economic issues related to education interventions (pp. 27–28).

- A **cost analysis** "is a method of economic evaluation that provides a complete accounting of the economic costs of a given intervention over and above the baseline scenario."
- A **cost-effectiveness analysis** is "a method of economic evaluation in which outcomes of an intervention are measured in nonmonetary terms. The outcomes and costs are compared with both the outcomes and cost for competing interventions (or an established standard) to determine whether the outcomes are achieved at reasonable monetary cost."
- A **cost-benefit analysis** is "a method of economic evaluation in which both costs and outcomes of an intervention are valued in monetary terms, permitting a direct comparison of the benefits produced by the intervention with its costs."
- An **economic return on investment analysis** is a cost-benefit analysis undertaken from the perspective of a specific stakeholder such as a school district.

In this report, we provide cost information that speaks to the affordability of the PPI along with academic ROI, which is a type of cost-effectiveness analysis. A district can use the cost information to understand "what it takes" to implement principal pipelines and assess whether that bottom line is affordable. The academic ROI results speak to whether the costs are reasonable in view of available information about other interventions. A district can use this information to understand how total PPI expenditures described on a per-student basis could translate into outcomes such as improvements in student achievement and principal retention. Districts can compare this information with information about other interventions to determine whether the PPI seems like a good investment. In the cost-effectiveness analysis, we are limited by the availability of other studies that include an economic analysis of similar education interventions. We did not feel comfortable taking the next step of translating the effects we measured into monetary terms, because it would have involved making assumptions about the long-run implications of improvements in students' academic achievement.

PPI, and thus subject to all of the previously mentioned limitations of that analysis. Second, our estimate assumes that our collected cost data, by and large, capture the total expenditures by districts on pipeline-related activities. Some inaccuracy in our estimate is therefore possible, to the extent that we failed to document any PPI-related expenditures that contributed to causal impacts, or to the extent that our cost estimates include expenditures that did not directly contribute to the PPI. As is the case for our estimates of the effects of the PPI, it is difficult to identify which specific investments may have made the most impact.

Summary

Our study approach was designed to provide a comprehensive description of the implementation and effects of the efforts of the six districts that implemented principal pipelines. Our main approach for estimating PPI effects compared changes in achievement and other outcomes in schools that receive newly placed principals in these PPI districts to similar schools with newly placed principals in other districts in the state. We also applied this approach in a rigorous analysis of effects for subgroups of schools. Separately, we used an exploratory methodology—with important limitations—in an effort to try to disentangle the effects on achievement of different pipeline components.

CHAPTER THREE

Implementation of the Principal Pipeline Initiative

In this chapter, we describe what the PPI districts were able to accomplish and provide some insights into how they did so and what these accomplishments meant for principals in these districts. We describe the actions districts took to revise policies, procedures, and processes related to the management of principals. We also describe the characteristics and experiences of newly placed principals in PPI districts and how those changed over time. We begin with an overview of the starting point for implementation.

District Policies, Procedures, and Practices

As described in Turnbull, Anderson, et al. (2016), the PPI outlined expectations for each of the pipeline components:

- Districts would adopt standards of professional practice and performance and use those standards in shaping policies related to school leader preparation, hiring, placement, and support.
- Preservice preparation would be provided by one or more of the following: university partners, nonprofit partners, and in-house district programs. The district would play a substantial role in shaping the programs. Preparation would include on-the-job training involving a long-term clinical experience. Admission to and the content of preservice preparation would be aligned with the district's leadership standards and competencies.
- Districts would use a multi-stage selective hiring and placement practice to match principal candidates with school vacancies. The selection process would collect and rely on information about capabilities related to district leader standards.
- Evaluation and support for novice principals would be aligned to standards. Districts would systematically assess principals' instructional leadership capabilities over their first three years on the job and provide feedback and support toward meeting expectations.

We assessed the degree to which each district had implemented each component at the start of the initiative and then as the initiative was winding down based on the following criteria. A district is said to have implemented the component if all criteria are met:

- **Standards**
  - District has standards of principal practice
  - District standards are used in any pipeline process
- **Preservice Training**
  - Most principals appointed by the district are graduates of a partner or district-run program.
  - Partner and district-run programs include on-the-job training through a clinical experience and are aligned with district standards.
- **Selective Hiring**
  - The selection process includes entry into a talent or hiring pool
  - Candidates are required to complete performance tasks aligned to district standards as part of the hiring process.
- **Evaluation and Support**
  - The district implemented a standards-based evaluation system
  - Novice principals receive support through a mentor or coach.

We characterized a district as having partially implemented the component if only one of the two criteria was met and as having fully implemented the component if both criteria were met. Comparing the characterization between the two time points provides a sense of the degree of change with the following caveats. A district could make substantial progress toward certain criteria but not quite reach them. For example, a district could have increased the share of new hires who had attended a partner or district-run preservice training program but not up to the threshold. Similarly, a district could improve upon implementation even after meeting the criteria. For example, districts that had standards at the beginning of the initiative, revisited and refined them during the initiative.

Starting Point (Pre-PPI)

All six PPI districts had some pipeline components at least partially in place at the start of the initiative (Figure 3.1). The superintendents of the PPI districts affirmed a commitment to school leadership as a lever for school improvement and agreed to implement the four components of the PPI and the systems and capacity needed to sustain the work over time. District superintendents were asked to commit to engagement in PPI efforts throughout the initiative and were expected to attend two PPI professional learning community meetings per year. While all districts planned improvements in each of the four PPI components, three of the districts (A, D and E) already had imple-

Figure 3.1
District Experience with Pipeline Components as of SY 2010–2011 (Pre-PPI)

PPI Component	District A	District B	District C	District D	District E	District F
1. Leader standards	Component in place	Component not in place	Component partially in place	Component in place	Component partially in place	Component partially in place
2. Preservice training	Component in place	Component partially in place	Component partially in place	Component partially in place	Component in place	Component partially in place
3. Selective hiring	Component in place	Component not in place	Component partially in place	Component not in place	Component in place	Component partially in place
4. Evaluation and support	Component partially in place	Component partially in place	Component partially in place	Component in place	Component partially in place	Component partially in place

☐ Component not in place ▒ Component partially in place ■ Component in place

mented the intended systems corresponding to one or more PPI components and two of those districts (A and E) had all components at least partially in place. The other three districts (B, C and F) had not fully implemented the intended systems corresponding to any of the PPI components, suggesting that they had the most room to grow during the PPI. In the school year prior to the launch of the initiative (SY 2010–2011):

- Some, but not all, of the districts had leader standards in place. These continued to evolve over the course of the study period, however.
- All the districts had a partnership with at least one preservice provider that it considered to be "preferred" and therefore had the preservice training component at least partially in place. Preferred providers were district-run programs in some cases and programs run by universities or non-profit organizations in other cases.
- Some of the districts had a systematic screening process for new hires.
- Some of the districts had a standards-based evaluation system in place.
- All the districts had mentoring for new principal hires and therefore had the evaluation and support component at least partially in place.[1]

Status of District Efforts as of School Year 2016–2017

District experience with pipeline components evolved during the PPI. The three districts (B, C, and F) that had not fully implemented the intended systems corresponding to any of the PPI components in SY 2010–2011 had between two and four components in place by SY 2016–2017 and the others partially in place. By the end of the

[1] Districts varied in whether they used the term *mentoring* or *coaching* for individual support; some had cadres of both mentors and coaches. Because there was no uniform definition of either term across districts, we use *mentoring* for simplicity in this report.

initiative, all districts had all components at least partially in place. All districts had leader standards in place and were using them to drive other components of the pipeline (Figure 3.2). All districts had developed LTSs—databases with comprehensive information about current and aspiring leaders and district schools—and were using these data to inform pipeline activities. Early in the initiative, all six districts made significant revisions to their hiring and placement efforts, using data to drive decisions and ensuring that interview and screening processes included enhanced practical demonstrations of competencies, rather than just interviews. By the end of the initiative, each district had a district-run principal preparation program for high-potential assistant principals in the district. They also were engaging with external preservice providers to ensure that the programs were meeting district needs. In particular, all PPI districts undertook efforts to enhance clinical experiences in both in-house and external programs. All of the districts had also implemented a standards-based evaluation system and therefore had the evaluation and support component fully in place.

While PPI districts approached pipeline implementation in different ways, there were common elements across the six sites as of the start of SY 2016–2017, which is when our monitoring of implementation ended:

- adoption of leader standards and use of those standards to inform other components of the pipeline
- development of an LTS
- strategic hiring and placement using data from LTSs
- use of practical demonstrations of competencies in the hiring process for principals
- establishment of a district-run principal preparation program for high-potential assistant principals, and establishment of working relationships with university preparation programs
- continued provision of mentoring support for novice principals
- use of leader standards in principal evaluation.

Figure 3.2
Status of Pipeline Components as of SY 2016–2017 (End of the PPI)

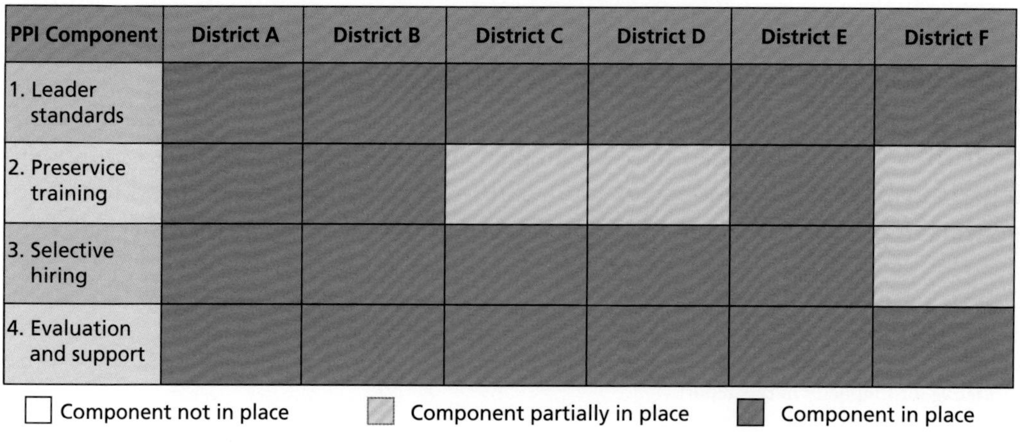

PPI Component	District A	District B	District C	District D	District E	District F
1. Leader standards	in place	in place	in place	in place	in place	in place
2. Preservice training	in place	in place	partially in place	partially in place	in place	partially in place
3. Selective hiring	in place	in place	in place	in place	in place	partially in place
4. Evaluation and support	in place	in place	in place	in place	in place	in place

☐ Component not in place   ▨ Component partially in place   ■ Component in place

All Six Districts Undertook Improvements to Pipeline Activities During the Initiative
Kaufman, Gates, et al. (2017) developed a list of pipeline activities and subactivities that PPI districts undertook in each component. These are described in Text Box 3.1. During the PPI, districts improved the activities that are part of the principal pipeline.

Pipeline Enhancement Efforts Had Some Important Differences
While all districts undertook improvements to the pipeline activities during the initiative, they had important flexibility regarding how they went about them. PPI districts differed in terms of how they allocated their pipeline resources. While preservice preparation and on-the-job support consumed the majority of resources, districts differed in terms of the relative emphasis between the two. Districts used vastly different approaches to support preservice. Some had a district-run program that was essentially required for aspiring principals. Several had a district-run program and partnerships with different numbers of external providers (the range of approaches is described in depth in Turnbull, Riley, and MacFarlane, 2013). Districts also differed in terms of how they shared the cost of preservice preparation with aspiring principals (see Kaufman, Gates, et al., 2017, p. 49). The three districts that were characterized as partially implementing the preservice component as of SY 2016–2017 were so designated because *some* but not *most* of their new hires had completed a program run by the district or a partner.

During the PPI, preferred preservice providers in three of the districts dramatically expanded the clinical aspect of their programs (Turnbull, Anderson, et al., 2016, p. 19). Other districts supported clinical experiences for preservice programs of external providers. While all districts undertook efforts to enhance the quality of preservice clinical experience, they experimented with different approaches for selecting sites and mentors and structuring the clinical experiences. In some cases, clinical experiences, under the guidance of a supervisor or mentor principal, were provided in the context of a candidate's current position. Alternatively, the clinical experience takes place in a new setting—an option that is usually referred to as a "residency" for a school leader candidate. The duration of the residency for preservice programs in PPI districts varied from a month to an entire school year (Turnbull, Anderson, et al., 2016, p. 19).

All PPI districts devoted substantial resources to on-the-job support, but the specific approaches varied widely, both across districts and within districts over time, in terms of the emphasis placed on support in the first year versus later years, the type of support (mentoring, professional development), relative emphasis on principals versus assistant principals, and use of specific tools or techniques, such as the National SAM Innovation project (a professional development program designed to help principals manage their time more effectively and devote more time to instructional leadership).

This variation is reflected in variation in expenditures as described below.

Text Box 3.1. Principal Pipeline Activities

Component 1: Leader Standards

- Develop or revise leader standards and secure their approval.

Component 2: Preservice Preparation

- Revise system of preservice recruitment, selection, and preparation.
    - Develop internal, district-led preservice courses.
    - Develop external, program- or university-based courses.
    - Develop screening and selection processes.
    - Prepare/train personnel to use new screening/selection processes.
- Recruit principal and AP candidates for preservice preparation.
- Screen and select candidates for preservice preparation.
- Deliver preservice preparation.
    - Deliver internal, district-led preparation.
    - Deliver external, contractor-/partner-led preparation.
- Oversee quality of portfolio of preservice preparation programs.

Component 3: Selective Hiring and Placement

- Revise system for principal recruiting, hiring, and placement (design processes and train personnel).
- Recruit principal and AP candidates.
- Screen, select, and support candidate pool.
- Interview and hire school leaders.

Component 4: On-the-Job Evaluation and Support

- Revise system for providing on-the-job support and evaluation for principals and APs.
    - Design new on-the-job support/induction processes and courses and provide personnel training.
    - Design new evaluation processes, including technology, and provide personnel training.
- Provide on-the-job support/induction for principals and APs.
    - Provide induction and first year on-the-job professional development.
    - Provide on-the-job professional development after the first year.
    - Provide school-wide support via teams and networks.
- Evaluate principals and APs.
- Provide executive coaching and support to those who supervise and support principals.

Systems and Capacity for Supporting the Pipeline Components

- Revise the overall principal pipeline.
- Develop and disseminate communication about the PPI.
- Develop and maintain LTS.
- Oversee implementation of pipeline (quality assurance).
- Separate activities for principals and assistant principals.

What Districts Spent on Their Pipeline Efforts

Kaufman, Gates, et al. (2017) examined the resources and expenditures associated with pipeline investments by the six PPI districts during the timeframe of the initiative. The study emphasized that many of the pipeline activities are standard district operating costs—things a district would do with or without an initiative like the PPI. It found that, on average over the course of the initiative, PPI districts spent 0.4 percent of the district budget each year (or $5.6 million dollars, $31,000 per principal in the district or $42 per pupil in the district) on pipeline activities. The cost of time for district personnel accounted for about half of these expenditures (44 percent), suggesting that the work requires a district commitment to allow staff—especially senior district staff—to dedicate their time to this work. Thirty percent of these expenditures were investments in pipeline enhancement, as opposed to ongoing costs of operating the pipelines.

Here we summarize some key findings from the study (see Kaufman, Gates, et al., 2017, pp. xvi–xviii). Figure 3.3 presents the average annual per-principal expenditures by PPI districts over the course of the initiative. The thick horizontal bars reflect the average expenditure and the vertical bars indicate the range of expenditures across districts. As reflected in the figure, spending on **leader standards** represented a very small share of total pipeline expenditures when averaged across districts ($29 per principal or $0.41 per pupil, as seen in Figure 3.3). Three districts emphasized leader standards work early in the initiative; two emphasized this work consistently over time, while one emphasized it later in the initiative.

Spending on **selective hiring and placement** and **systems and capacity (including LTSs)** was also relatively low with low variation across districts.

Spending on selective hiring and placement was $2,894 per principal in the district or $3.57 per pupil, and half of these expenditures were viewed by the districts as investments in revisions to hiring systems. Our analysis of the per-pupil expenditure estimates in the cost study data suggest that, of the five districts for which we have data, one had lower expenditures on selective hiring and placement than the others. A bulk of the investments in revisions to hiring systems occurred in SY 2013–2014 and earlier.

Spending on system and capacity was $3,425 per principal per year on average, with limited variation across districts, and with LTS development accounting for over half of those average expenditures.

Two pipeline components, preservice preparation and on-the-job support and evaluation, accounted for nearly three-quarters of pipeline expenditures and also had the greatest variation across districts and over time. Spending on **preservice preparation** amounted to $9,386 per principal[2] or $13.27 per pupil. While all districts spent a

---

[2]   As described in Kaufman, Gates, et al. (2017), this per-principal cost is the total district expenditures on preservice divided by the total number of principals in the district. It does not reflect the cost per participant in the preservice activities.

Figure 3.3
Average Annual Per-Principal Resources and Expenditures, by Major Category (2011–2012 Through 2014–2015)

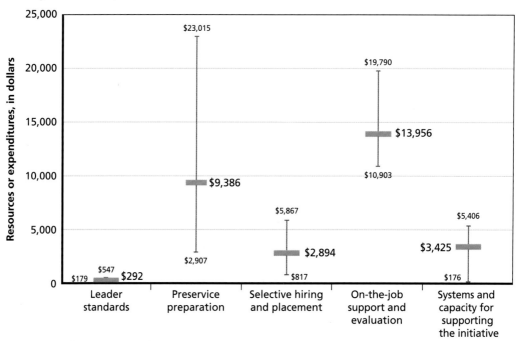

SOURCE: Kaufman, Gates, et al., 2017, Figure 3.1.
NOTE: Each estimate of overall average pipeline costs represents an average of the overall costs in each district. Because we have cost estimates for spending on only three of the five major pipeline categories for New York City, we do not include data for that city for the two missing categories (selective hiring and placement and on-the-job support and evaluation).

substantial share of pipeline resources on preservice preparation, they did so in different ways. One district emphasized preservice preparation for APs, three developed new in-house programs for candidates about to assume a principalship, and most districts invested in a range of options to meet diverse needs of aspiring leaders and managed those strategically. Over the course of the initiative, expenditures on preservice delivery rose in all but one district. As the PPI was launched, most districts were eager to enhance the pool of candidates for principal vacancies (Turnbull, Riley, Arcaira, et al., 2013). By 2015, most districts reported that they were satisfied with the quality of candidates, and some were discussing challenges associated with managing expectations for promising candidates for whom the district did not have a vacancy (Turnbull, Anderson, et al., 2016). Our in-depth analysis of the expenditures revealed that districts adopted vastly different approaches to funding and delivery of preservice preparation based on their local context, opportunities, and needs. Costs associated with residencies were associated with larger expenditures on preservice delivery. Over the course of the initiative, districts looked for ways to limit the cost of residencies while still ensuring a quality learning experience.

District expenditures for **on-the-job support** rose most sharply between SYs 2011–2012 and 2012–2013 in all districts for which we obtained data (Kaufman, Gates, et al., 2017, pp. 55–56), indicating that the first year of the PPI treatment is also the year when districts began to dedicate more resources to support. All districts provided support to principals and APs.[3] In supporting principals, all districts provided such support not only to first-year principals but also to those beyond their first year. Districts varied in terms of the extent to which this support was targeted to first-year principals or also included supports for veteran principals. Three of the districts spread on-the-job support resources across principals and APs and supported both first-year principals and more-experienced principals. Two of the districts devoted nearly all on-the-job support resources toward principals, with one of those districts devoting three-quarters toward first-year principals and the other devoting about half.

Number and Characteristics of Newly Placed Principals

Table 3.1 documents the number of newly placed principals by district and by school year. This total number includes new principal hires and reassigned principals (see Text Box 2.4 for definitions of these terms). As illustrated in Figure 3.4, districts varied in terms of the share of newly placed principals who were reassigned principals versus new principal hires.

Although it was not an explicit goal of the PPI to enhance diversity in the principal pipeline, we did examine whether there were any changes in the demographic characteristics of principals in PPI districts. Over the period of the study, we observed few notable changes in the demographic characteristics of newly placed principals. New principals' race, gender, and age were relatively unchanged over time. New principals were also relatively similar over time in terms of the number of years of teaching experience that they held prior to assuming the principalship.

Experiences

In its evaluation of the implementation of the PPI, PSA found that the hiring experiences and perceptions of new principal hires changed in meaningful ways during the initiative. Between 2013 and 2015, a larger share of new hires reported an excellent fit between their strengths and the needs of their school and reported that they had been subject to practical demonstrations in the application and hiring process and received feedback during the hiring process (see Turnbull, Anderson, et al., 2016, pp. 29–33). District leaders reported that changes to the hiring systems were successful and that they viewed new principal hires favorably (Turnbull, Anderson, et al., 2016).

---

[3] Although PPI districts did provide support for APs as part of the PPI, this report focuses on outcomes for principals.

Table 3.1
Number of Newly Placed Principals, by District and School Year

School District	2010–2011	2011–2012	2012–2013	2013–2014	2014–2015	2015–2016	2016–2017
Charlotte	37	54	26	34	57	26	34
Denver	27	58	30	47	30	45	25
Gwinnett	23	24	25	28	17	19	20
Hillsborough	31	46	48	58	46	52	41
Prince George's	39	58	45	23	51	24	46
New York City	228	237	226	225	210	223	172
Total	385	477	400	415	411	389	338

SOURCE: RAND analysis of district-provided data.

Figure 3.4
Newly Placed Principals as a Percentage of All District Principals, by District and Principal Type

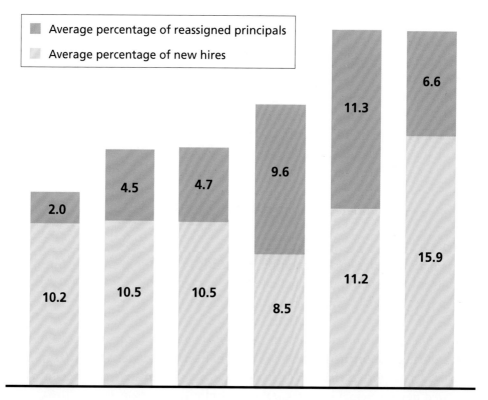

NOTE: Districts are presented in order from lowest to highest in terms of the percentage of newly placed principals (new hires and transfers combined) among all principals.

Comparing survey responses from new principal hires who assumed a principalship between March 2013 and February 2015 with those from principals who assumed a principalship between March 2010 and February 2012, PSA more specifically found the following:[4]

- 59 percent of new principal hires in the later period reported participating in practical demonstrations during the hiring process, up from 31 percent among those hired in the earlier time period, and the percentage reporting that they had received useful feedback in the process rose from 52 to 67 percent (Turnbull, Anderson, et al., 2016, p. 31).
- 72 percent of those hired in the later period reported an excellent fit between their skills, experiences, and interests and the needs of their school, up from 60 percent in the earlier period.[5]
- The later group of new principal hires also felt that their preparation was more focused on the principalship as a career. Forty-four percent reported that their preservice preparation gave them a strong orientation to the principalship as a career to a great extent, up from 31 percent in the earlier period.

Although PSA's analysis of 2013 and 2015 survey responses found no other differences related to preservice, a follow-up survey conducted in 2018 did (Anderson and Turnbull, 2019, p. 13).[6] That survey, conducted after the end of the initiative, found that principals whose preservice preparation began after March 2012 reported different experiences than those who had completed their preparation by that time. Specifically, these principals who had begun preservice after the PPI was underway reported that their programs had a greater emphasis on instructional leadership, school improvement and tailoring to district context. However, given the median time lag between starting preservice and being hired as a principal, which ranged from four to nine years for PPI districts, few of those who started preservice after March 2012 would have become principals early enough for any effects on their schools to be measured during the timeframe of this evaluation study.

Separately, in our analysis of principals' LTS data, we observed that two out of the six districts had notable increases in the percentage of new principal hires who were

---

[4] The 2013 survey had 353 respondents and an overall response rate of 57 percent. The 2015 survey had 514 respondents and an overall response rate of 65 percent.

[5] New principals' self-reported fit with their schools was no longer trending upward in the 2018 survey described later in this section, however. Among those on the job for two years or fewer in 2018, 63 percent reported an "excellent" fit, a percentage that falls between those who gave that response in 2013 and 2015 and is not significantly different from either.

[6] The 2018 survey had 979 respondents and an overall response rate of 68 percent. The 2018 survey included veteran principals as well as novice principals. The weighted number of novice principals (those on the job for two years or less) in the 2018 survey is 217.

trained in a preferred preservice program between SYs 2010–2011 and 2016–2017 (while a third district hired all principals from its preferred program throughout the study period). The remaining three districts did not hire more from preferred preservice programs over the period of the study. That said, because preservice programs take time to develop new graduates, we do not know whether changes in these districts may be forthcoming in future school years.

District-wide reforms to systems related to leader standards, selective hiring, and principal evaluation also affected all new principal hires (a term that includes both novice principals and also veteran principals new to the district) during the study period. For example, leader standards were used to define goals for all principals' practice and were referenced in hiring, evaluation, and support systems. Hiring systems affected all new principals in the sense that they determined which types of principals were and were not hired.

Finally, in the area of induction support provided to principals, most new district hires in PPI districts experienced mentoring and/or professional development supports in their first few years on the job. In particular, all six districts reported that they had some kind of mentoring system in place to support new principals throughout the period of the study. At the individual principal level, districts' LTSs varied in terms of which specific professional development and mentoring activities were documented with fidelity. Overall, however, for most districts (five out of six) we observe increases over the period of this study in the proportion of new principals for whom induction mentoring and/or professional development were documented.[7]

Summary

All six large urban districts that were part of the PPI made progress to improve the way they were doing the pipeline activities. They all had different starting points, faced different opportunities and constraints, and went about the work in different ways. At the start of the initiative, three of the districts (A, D, and E) already had implemented the intended systems corresponding to one or more PPI components and two of those districts (A and E) had every component at least partially in place. The other three districts (B, C, and F) had more room to grow during the PPI because they had not fully implemented the intended systems corresponding to any of the PPI components. By SY 2016–2017, those three districts had between two and four components in place and the others partially in place.

---

[7]   Several districts also supported the National SAM Innovation project– a professional development program— and documented individuals' participation in that program via their LTSs. SAM participation fluctuated over the period of the study, with some districts having increased numbers of principals participating and others with fewer participants over time.

Even when districts had a component in place as of SY 2010–2011, they worked to improve their implementation of the component over the course of the PPI. For example, they refined their leader standards, adjusted preservice training, revised hiring practices, and revisited induction supports.

These pipeline efforts changed the experiences of new principal hires in PPI districts. Over time, a larger share of new hires was subject to practical demonstrations in the application and hiring process and reported receiving feedback during the hiring process. There is also evidence that principals whose preservice preparation began after the PPI was under way reported that their programs had a greater emphasis on instructional leadership, school improvement and tailoring to district context compared with those who completed preservice preparation earlier. In two out of the six PPI districts, there were notable increases in the percentage of new principal hires who were trained in a preferred preservice program between SYs 2010–2011 and 2016–2017. And in most PPI districts we observed increases in the proportion of new principals for whom induction mentoring and/or professional development were documented.

CHAPTER FOUR

Effects of the Principal Pipeline Initiative

In this chapter, we present the estimated effects of the PPI on key outcomes of interest: student achievement, principal retention, and other student and school outcomes. We also discuss findings from the exploratory analysis relating PPI effects to exposure to pipeline components and to school characteristics. The effects we highlight are statistically significantly different at the 5-percent level.

Student Achievement

Schools in PPI Districts That Received a Newly Placed Principal Outperformed Comparison Schools

As described in Chapter Two, to characterize the primary PPI effect, we focused on schools that received a newly placed principal after SY 2011–2012 and compared their outcomes to those of schools in non-PPI districts that also received a new principal. Figure 4.1 presents our findings. These schools in PPI districts outperformed comparison schools by 6.22 percentile points in reading and 2.87 percentile points in mathematics three or more years after the placement of a new principal (Figure 4.1). After two years, schools that received a new principal in PPI districts outperformed similar schools in non-PPI districts by 4.96 and 2.61 percentile points in reading and mathematics, respectively. Apparent differences between the two-year and three-or-more-year results are not statistically significant from one another. The results are of a magnitude that is sizable. In other words, our results suggest that a school that received a new principal and whose students would have otherwise been at the median (50th percentile) in reading achievement without the PPI instead would have reading achievement scores above the 56th percentile as a result of the PPI.

It is challenging to relate these findings to those of other education evaluations that have a district-wide scope and aim at school-wide effects. We found no other district-wide intervention comparable to the PPI for which there is evidence of positive effects. Recently, Stecher et al. (2018) found that the Intensive Partnerships for Effective Teaching initiative did not achieve its goals of improving teacher effectiveness or student outcomes in the districts that implemented it. An evaluation of New Leaders'

Figure 4.1
In Schools in PPI Districts That Received a Newly Placed Principal, the Change in Student Achievement in Both Math and Reading Was Substantially Better than in Comparison Schools

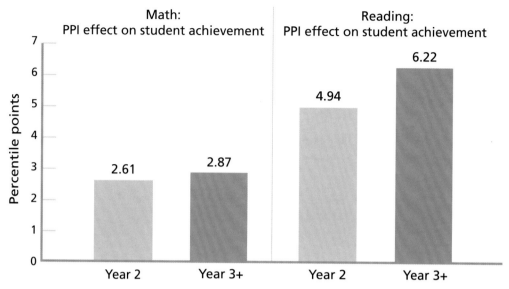

NOTES: The numerals indicate the *PPI effect* on student achievement: the difference between the percentile point change in achievement for schools in PPI districts and similar schools in other districts. The change in achievement is measured here between the baseline year (SY 2010–2011) and either two or three+ years after the placement of a new principal. These effects are statistically significant at the 5-percent level.

Aspiring Principals program that serves a subset of schools within districts found that after three or more years, achievement in schools that received a New Leaders principal was 3.26 to 3.55 percentile points higher in mathematics and 1.81 to 2.27 percentile points higher in English language arts than achievement in schools that received a new principal in the same district who was not a New Leader (Gates et. al., 2019). The effects measured in that evaluation, which used within-district comparisons, apply to the subset of students who are in schools that have a principal who completed the Aspiring Principals program. Other points of comparison based on student, classroom, or school-wide interventions also may be relevant. For example, What Works Clearinghouse (WWC) reports that teachers trained by Teach for America improve the achievement of students in their classrooms by 4 percentile points in mathematics relative to comparison teachers (U.S. Department of Education, 2018c). Teach for America is similar to the PPI in that it is implemented district-wide in districts that partner with the organization, but its evaluations are different in that the effects are measured for students within the classrooms of participating teachers. Similarly, WWC reports that the Knowledge is Power Program (KIPP)—a program operated by a CMO—has an 8-percentile-point increase for reading and 12 for mathematics—effects that are measured for students who attend a KIPP charter school (U.S. Department of Education, 2016).

We also analyzed the effects of the PPI on all schools district-wide, not only those that received a newly placed principal. As discussed earlier, we did this because some of the initiative's components could plausibly improve the overall performance of sitting principals, whether directly by supporting them or indirectly by helping the district pinpoint and replace its less effective principals. We found that the effects of the PPI on school-level mathematics and reading achievement for all schools in the district (as opposed to only schools with newly placed principals) as of SY 2012–2013 are similar to the main effects, but mostly smaller in magnitude. The lighter-shaded bars in Figure 4.2 summarize these effects for all schools in the district as of SY 2012–2013. As a point of comparison, we also present the effects for the newly placed principals in SY 2012–2013 (right, darker bars). The district-wide effects are 5.01 percentile points

Figure 4.2
Relative to Comparison Schools, Changes in Student Achievement Were More Positive in all Schools in PPI Districts—Not Just Those That Received a Newly Placed Principal

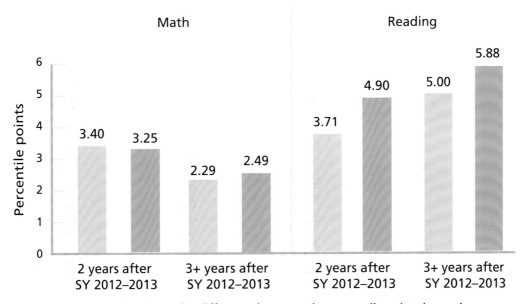

NOTES: The numerals indicate the difference between the percentile point change in achievement for schools in PPI districts and similar schools in other districts. The change in achievement is measured here between the baseline year (SY 2010–2011) and either two or three+ years after SY 2012–2013. Lighter bars show the effects for all schools in PPI districts, and darker bars show the effects for schools in PPI districts that received a newly placed principal in SY 2012–2013. These effects are statistically significant at the 5-percent level.

in reading and 2.29 percentile points in mathematics after three or more years, and 3.71 percentile points in reading and 3.40 percentile points in mathematics after two years. Schools in PPI districts that received a newly placed principal in the 2012–2013 school year outperformed schools in other districts that received a newly placed principal in that year by 5.88 percentile points in reading and 2.49 percentile points in mathematics after three or more years and by 4.90 percentile points in reading and 3.25 percentile points in mathematics after two years. All of these findings are statistically significant at the 5-percent level.

Next, we discuss findings from some subgroup analyses. We present subgroup effects for schools led by newly placed principals. Unless otherwise noted, the subgroup analyses are as rigorous as the main analysis, but because they involve smaller samples, they often have less power to detect statistically significant effects.

We Found Positive PPI Effects on Achievement for Elementary and Middle Schools

When we examined PPI effects on achievement for elementary schools, middle schools, and high schools separately, we found evidence of positive PPI effects at all grade levels, shown in Figure 4.3. The estimated treatment effects are larger and consistently posi-

Figure 4.3
The PPI Effect on Student Achievement Was Positive Across Elementary and Middle Schools

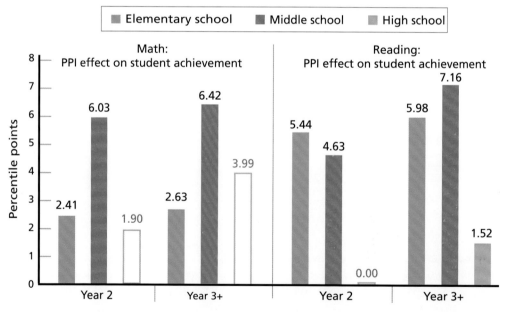

NOTES: The numerals indicate the *PPI effect* on student achievement: the difference between the percentile point change in achievement for schools in PPI districts and similar schools in other districts. The change in achievement is measured here between the baseline year (SY 2010–2011) and either two or three+ years after the placement of a new principal. These effects are statistically significant at the 5-percent level, except for the high school math effect for year 2 and year 3+ and the high school reading effect for year 2; these three effects are shown with hollow (white) bars and gray numerals.

tive and statistically significant for elementary and middle schools. At the high school level, the PPI effect is positive and statistically significant only for mathematics after three or more years.

District-by-District Estimates of the Effect of the PPI on Student Achievement Varied but Were Mostly Positive

District-by-district estimates of PPI effects lent further support for the overall findings. As illustrated in Figure 4.4, point estimates were positive across the board in reading. The estimated size of the effects varied by district from under 1 percentile point to nearly 20 percentile points. They are statistically significant for five of the six districts after three or more years. Figure 4.5 shows the results for mathematics by district. Here, we saw more variation by district. The results for three or more years are positive and statistically significant for three districts, estimated as between 4.5 and 10 percentile points. Results in mathematics were negative and statistically significant for one district, where the year-three-plus estimate was nearly –7 percentile points. In two districts, the estimates were positive but not statistically significant. Further explora-

Figure 4.4
The PPI Effect on Student Achievement in Reading After Three or More Years Was Positive in Five of the Six PPI Districts

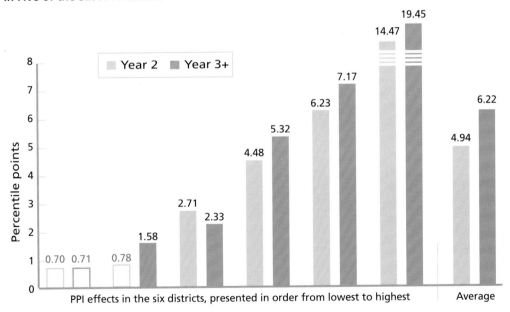

NOTES: The numerals indicate the *PPI effect* on student achievement: the difference between the percentile point change in achievement for schools in PPI districts and similar schools in other districts. The change in achievement is measured here between the baseline year (SY 2010–2011) and either two or three+ years after the placement of a new principal, for each district. District results are presented in order from lowest to highest. These effects are statistically significant at the 5-percent level, except for the three left-most effects, which are shown with hollow (white) bars and gray numerals.

Figure 4.5
The PPI Effect on Student Achievement in Math Was Positive in Three of the Six PPI Districts and Negative in One District

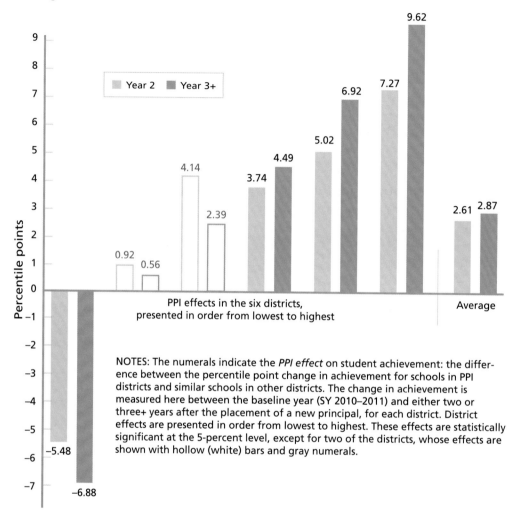

NOTES: The numerals indicate the *PPI effect* on student achievement: the difference between the percentile point change in achievement for schools in PPI districts and similar schools in other districts. The change in achievement is measured here between the baseline year (SY 2010–2011) and either two or three+ years after the placement of a new principal, for each district. District effects are presented in order from lowest to highest. These effects are statistically significant at the 5-percent level, except for two of the districts, whose effects are shown with hollow (white) bars and gray numerals.

tion through by-district and by-grade-level analysis (not shown here) revealed that the negative effects found in one district were found only in its elementary schools.

The three districts that had the most room to grow during the PPI (that is, the ones that had not fully implemented the intended systems corresponding to any of the PPI components prior to the PPI) all had positive outcomes that are statistically significant in one or both subjects.

Effects of the PPI on Achievement Were Evident Even for the Earliest Cohorts of PPI Schools

To examine the timing of PPI effects, we estimated effects by cohort, defined in terms of the year in which a school received a newly placed principal. Our findings suggest that the benefits of the PPI kicked in quickly. As reflected in Figure 4.6, when we looked at effects by cohort for all newly placed principals, we found positive and statistically significant effects for all cohorts, including the earliest ones.

As illustrated by Figure 4.7, when we looked exclusively at new principal hires, we found that here too, effects on student achievement were statistically significant for all cohorts including the earliest ones and remained steady for subsequent cohorts, perhaps even increasing slightly for reading. The trends for reassigned principals on the other hand are mixed and not always statistically significant (see Figure D.5 in Appendix D).

Figure 4.6
The PPI Effect on Student Achievement Was Positive for Schools That Received a Newly Placed Principal in Each Year from SY 2012–2013 to SY 2015–2016

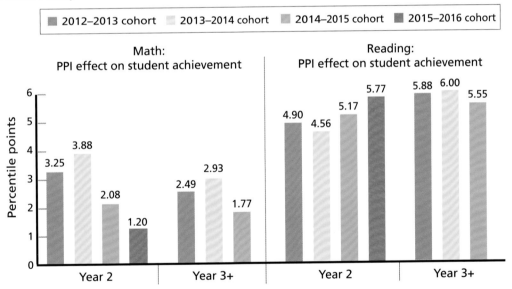

NOTES: The numerals indicate the *PPI effect* on student achievement: the difference between the percentile point change in achievement for schools in PPI districts and similar schools in other districts. The change in achievement is measured here between the baseline year (SY 2010–2011) and either two or three+ years after the placement of a new principal, and the effects are broken down by cohort, defined in terms of the year in which a school received a newly placed principal. These effects are statistically significant at the 5-percent level.

Figure 4.7

The PPI Effect On Student Achievement Was Positive for Schools That Received a Newly Hired Principal in Each Year from SY 2012–2013 to SY 2015–2016

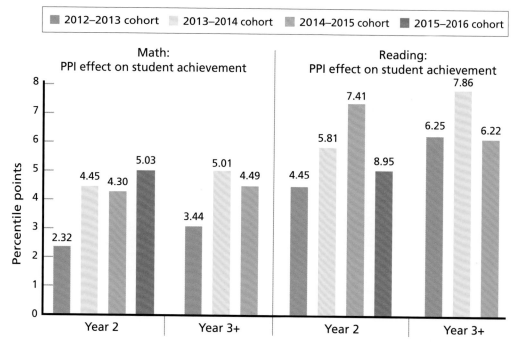

NOTES: The numerals indicate the *PPI effect* on student achievement: the difference between the percentile point change in achievement for schools in PPI districts and similar schools in other districts. The change in achievement is measured here between the baseline year (SY 2010–2011) and either two or three+ years after a new principal hire, and the effects are broken down by cohort, defined in terms of the SY in which the new principal was hired. These effects are statistically significant at the 5-percent level.

Effects of the PPI Were Positive for Schools in the Lowest Quartile of the Achievement Distribution

We conducted a subgroup analysis focused on schools serving students in different quartiles of the statewide distribution and schools serving high proportions (more than 50 percent and more than 75 percent) of non-white students and high proportions (more than 50 percent and more than 75 percent) of students eligible for free and reduced-price lunch. We selected these groupings because they are commonly used by the U.S. Department of Education to characterize schools as high-minority or high-poverty in reporting.

As illustrated in Figure 4.8, we found positive and statistically significant effects of the pipeline for schools with pre-PPI achievement in the lowest quartile of the state-wide distribution—those most likely to be identified for turnaround. The effects are smallest for schools with baseline achievement in the second-lowest quartile of the distribution (in mathematics) and the highest quartile (in reading). Differences in effect

Figure 4.8
The PPI Effect on Student Achievement Was Positive for Schools in the Lowest Quartile of Baseline Student Achievement

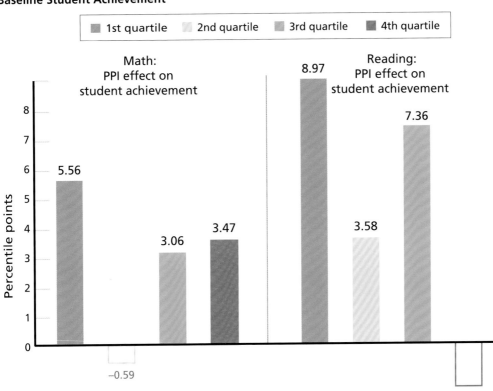

NOTES: The numerals indicate the *PPI effect* on student achievement: the difference between the percentile point change in achievement for schools in PPI districts and similar schools in other districts. The change in achievement is measured here between the baseline year (SY 2010–2011) and three+ years after the placement of a new principal, and the effects are broken down by average student achievement in the baseline year, with baseline student achievement divided into quartiles of the statewide achievement distribution. These effects are statistically significant at the 5-percent level, except for 2nd-quartile achievement in math and 4th-quartile achievement in reading; these results are shown with hollow (white) bars and gray text. Also, the difference between 1st-quartile and 2nd-quartile effects *is* statistically significant (not shown here but discussed in Appendix D).

sizes between the lowest and second-lowest quartile are statistically significant in both reading and mathematics.

Differences in the size of estimated effects across schools serving higher and lower proportions of non-white students and students eligible for free and reduced-price lunch were not statistically significant. The estimated effects were positive for all these subgroups (see Figures D.8 and D.9 in Appendix D).

Effects on Achievement May Be Larger for Schools That Receive a New Principal Hire

Figure 4.9 presents PPI effects on student achievement for new principal hires (those who are new to the principalship or to the district) and reassigned principals (those moving from another principalship in the district). This subgroup analysis should be viewed with caution, because within the comparison group we could not distinguish between the schools that had new principal hires and reassigned principals. Instead, outcomes in each subgroup of schools in the PPI districts are compared with outcomes for all newly placed principals in the comparison schools. When we looked specifically at the PPI effects on student achievement for new principal hires, the point estimates

Figure 4.9
The PPI Effect on Student Achievement May Be Greater for Schools That Receive a New Principal Hire Rather Than a Reassigned Principal

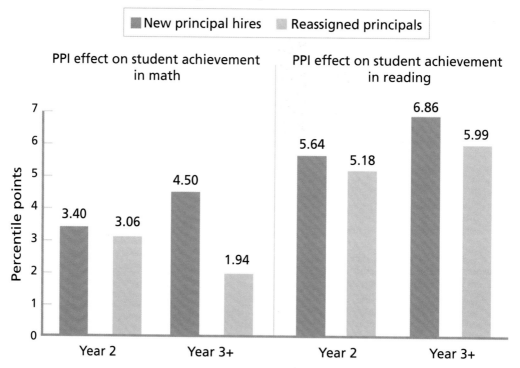

NOTES: The numerals indicate the *PPI effect* on student achievement: the difference between the percentile point change in achievement for schools in PPI districts and similar schools in other districts. The change in achievement is measured here between the baseline year (SY 2010–2011) and two or three+ years after the placement of a new principal, and the effects are broken down by whether the newly placed principals in the PPI districts were new hires or reassigned from other principalships in the district. A caveat is that, for the comparison group, we could not identify the subgroups of schools that had new principal hires or reassigned principals, so here we compare the outcomes for the PPI subgroups against outcomes for all newly placed principals in the comparison schools. These effects are statistically significant at the 5-percent level.

of effects are consistently larger than for schools that receive a reassigned principal, although the differences are not statistically significant. After two years, schools in PPI districts that received a new principal hire outperform comparison schools by 3.40 percentile points in mathematics and 5.64 percentile points in reading. After three or more years, treated schools that received a new principal hire outperform comparison schools by 4.50 percentile points in mathematics and 6.86 percentile points in reading.

What Do These Achievement Effects Mean?

Our analysis indicates that the PPI had a positive effect on achievement for schools that received a newly placed principal in SY 2012–2013 or later. We also found that the PPI benefited schools district-wide. The effects were widespread. We found evidence of positive PPI effects on achievement across all but one of the PPI districts. That said, we also found negative PPI effects on mathematics achievement in one of the PPI districts and no statistically significant effects on mathematics achievement in two districts. This variation suggests that the PPI does not have guaranteed results. Because we measured PPI effects relative to the "pre-PPI baseline" year of SY 2010–2011, our measures cannot account for effects of pipeline activities that were evident prior to the PPI. This could account for some of the variation we observed in district effects as well. Indeed, the three districts that had less of the pipeline in place in SY 2010–2011—and hence the most room to grow during implementation—had positive, statistically significant effects of the PPI.

PPI effects were strongest for elementary and middle schools, but we also found evidence of positive PPI effects in mathematics at the high school level. Weaker findings among high schools are not surprising given the small number of high schools with new principals in our sample. Also, the more complex career path to the high school principalship suggests that it might take a longer time for district efforts to influence high school principals.

We found that positive PPI effects are largest for schools with pre-PPI achievement in the lowest quartile of the distribution. This may reflect efforts on the part of several of the PPI districts to target turnaround schools and prioritize principal placements and other school supports in schools at the lower tier of the distribution. These findings suggest that those efforts may have been successful. However, they point to a need for districts to pay attention to the somewhat better-performing schools that are nevertheless below the state median, where we found weaker effects.

Our analysis also indicated that the effects of the pipeline kicked in right away. Positive effects were evident for the earliest cohorts of treated schools. This is consistent with the pattern of PPI implementation: Districts made early investments in induction support for first-year principals and then expanded that support in the second year while beefing up hiring processes.

We considered the possibility that other district-wide efforts could explain our findings.

Five of the six PPI districts were located in states that received Race to the Top funding. About half of this funding was distributed to districts across the states and the rest was used at the state level for core initiatives. Although some PPI districts used Race to the Top funding to support leadership initiatives, there is no evidence that PPI districts benefited disproportionately relative to non-PPI districts from Race to the Top (U.S. Department of Education, 2015).

Four of the six PPI districts participated in the Measures of Effective Teaching study (see Kane et al., 2013). Participating districts allowed researchers to contact principals and teachers about participation in a random controlled trial study designed to assess factors related to teacher effectiveness. This participation occurred in SY 2010–2011—prior to launch of the PPI—and was limited in scale. In total, 284 schools participated in the study. There is no evidence that participation had district-wide implications for the PPI districts.

One of the PPI districts implemented a major initiative focused on effective teaching that was concurrent with the PPI. This district received $100 million in grant funding to support the implementation and was expected to devote a similar level of district resources to this effort as well. The initiative placed substantial demands on principals, requiring them to devote a large amount of time to teacher evaluation. It also may have had implications for school staffing and for the district budget (Sokol, 2015). Based on evaluation findings of that initiative (Stecher et al., 2018) it is unlikely this initiative contributed to the positive PPI findings.

One PPI district was very active in private fundraising—efforts that started prior to the PPI. That district received two relatively large grants totaling $20 million to support the development of a teacher evaluation system to align with new statewide evaluation requirements. The second grant provided resources starting in SY 2013–2014—overlapping with the later stages of the PPI—that were used in part to support teacher leadership (Engdahl, 2013; Torres, 2013). The other PPI districts implemented other initiatives or efforts that overlapped with the PPI, but none were particularly large relative to the size of the respective districts.

Overall, we find the prevalence of findings across districts, time, and school levels combined with the stronger effects observed in schools that get newly placed principals and especially new district hires to be persuasive evidence that the PPI rather than a set of other disparate factors is behind the effects we observe.

Finally, there is suggestive evidence that effects were stronger for new district hires than for principals who had been reassigned from other schools. This reinforces the view that the effects we observe are due to the PPI. New principal hires would have been hired by the districts as principals after the PPI was implemented, and several features of PPI treatment were specifically designed to affect principals around the time of entry to the position. Changes in hiring procedures, induction support, and the final stages of preparation for the principalship would have affected them more than reassigned principals. Although reassigned principals were placed in their new schools during the initiative and thus could have had the benefit of standards- and data-based decisionmaking on placement, their preparation and induction likely predated the changes introduced under the initiative. Our data also showed that reassigned principals tended to have been somewhat lower performing in their prior positions, compared with principals who were not reassigned.[1] If the districts had reassigned their higher performers, more positive effects might have appeared in those principals' new schools.

Retention

Our findings on principal retention lend further support for the theory that the PPI benefited participating districts.

Newly Placed Principals in PPI Districts Were More Likely to Remain in Their Schools

Newly placed principals in PPI districts were 5.8 percentage points more likely to remain in their school for two years and 7.8 percentage points more likely to remain in their school for three years than newly placed principals in similar comparison schools (Figure 4.10). That means that for every 100 newly placed principals, PPI districts had

Figure 4.10
Newly Placed Principals in PPI Districts Were More Likely to Remain in Their Schools

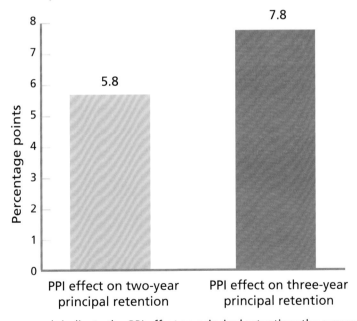

NOTES: The numerals indicate the *PPI effect* on principal retention: the percentage point difference between principal retention in PPI districts and similar schools in non-PPI districts. Retention is measured two and three years after the placement of a new principal. The effects here are statistically significant at the 5-percent level.

---

[1] This observation is based on our analysis of LTS data in districts that provided us with principal evaluation scores.

nearly six fewer losses after two years and nearly eight fewer losses after three years—implying that PPI districts are dealing with less churn in school leadership in the short run relative to comparable schools.

PPI Effects on Retention by District Show Mixed Effects

Unlike the effects on student achievement, which were quite consistent across districts, the effects of the PPI on retention across districts were more mixed. At the district level, where the analysis relies on smaller numbers and thus has less statistical power, retention effect estimates are statistically significant for only one district. As shown in Figure 4.11, PPI effects on retention were extremely positive and statistically significant in this district. Other district effects were not statistically significant but were moderately positive in three districts, near zero in one district and moderately negative in one district. The statistically significant positive retention estimates were observed in a district that also had positive achievement effects.

PPI Effects on Retention Are Larger for Later Cohorts of Newly Placed Principals and Possibly for New District Hires

Unlike the achievement effect, which was visible from the earliest cohorts of principals onward (Figure 4.6), the overall PPI effect on principal retention is larger for later cohorts. Figure D.6 in Appendix D shows the estimated treatment effects on principal retention by cohort. Notably, the three-year retention effect for the SY 2014–2015 cohort of newly placed principals (at 17 percentage points) was significantly larger (both statistically and substantively) than the three-year retention for the SY 2012–2013 cohort (at 1 percentage point).

Similar to the achievement findings (Figure 4.6), new principal hires show a larger estimated effect in terms of retention than reassigned principals, although the differences are not statistically significant. Figure D.7 in Appendix D shows the estimated treatment effects on principal retention for new district hires versus reassigned principals.

Discussion

We analyzed retention in the same school for two years and three years because if the comprehensive pipeline efforts were working well, districts would have a solid pool of candidates to choose from, would place them in schools that are a good match for their skills, and would be able to leave them in place for at least three years. PPI district officials agreed that this would be desirable. However, they also indicated that they sometimes had to move a well-performing principal out of initial placement after two years to serve in another school (perhaps with greater needs) or in another district role.[2] Our

---

[2]   During the PPI, several of the districts increased the number of principal supervisors and some districts intentionally pulled from the ranks of relatively new principals to fill those positions.

Figure 4.11
PPI Effects on Principal Retention for Each of the Six Districts Were Mixed

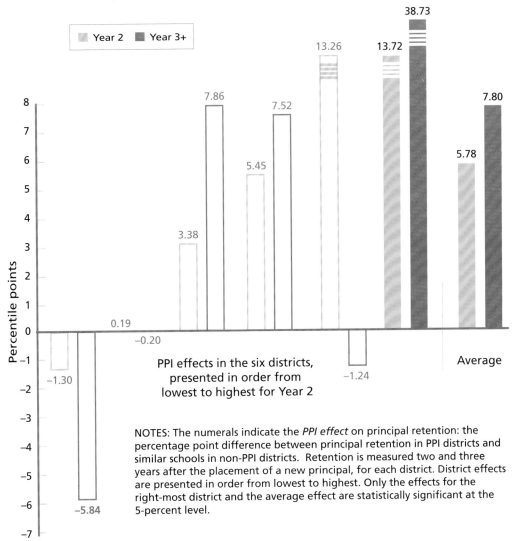

NOTES: The numerals indicate the *PPI effect* on principal retention: the percentage point difference between principal retention in PPI districts and similar schools in non-PPI districts. Retention is measured two and three years after the placement of a new principal, for each district. District effects are presented in order from lowest to highest. Only the effects for the right-most district and the average effect are statistically significant at the 5-percent level.

findings suggest that, overall, the retention of newly placed principals was better in PPI districts than in non-PPI districts, but also indicate variation in those outcomes across PPI districts. These findings are consistent with findings from the PPI sustainability report. District officials interviewed in the spring of 2018 reported that over time they had fewer principal vacancies and their new principal hires had stronger skills (Anderson and Turnbull, 2019).

Sensitivity Checks

Validating Assumption That, Absent the PPI, Outcomes for Schools in PPI Districts Would Have Followed the Trajectory of Outcomes Observed in Non-PPI Districts

Our main analytical approach relies on an assumption that, without the PPI, trends in outcomes of schools in PPI districts would be similar over time to the outcomes of similar schools in non-PPI districts. Analysts often validate this assumption by checking whether the trends are similar between treatment and comparison groups in the pretreatment period. This approach is called comparative interrupted time series (CITS). As a sensitivity check, we ran an analysis using a CITS approach. The results were qualitatively similar to those reported here. For the presentation of findings in this report, we chose the simpler difference-in-difference (DID) model rather than CITS. CITS makes assumptions that are not entirely consistent with the nature of the PPI intervention. The approach makes sense when there is a stable pre-treatment period of several years for which the analyst produces an estimate of the pre-treatment trend line. However, the fact that the districts selected for participation in the PPI had already undertaken some efforts to enhance principal pipelines means that our "pre-treatment" period is potentially contaminated by treatment. We would actually expect there to be a "pre-treatment" trend, which in and of itself would bias CITS estimates away from finding positive effects.

Alternative Starting Points for the PPI

We replicated the main analysis under alternative assumptions about when schools in PPI districts would experience effects of the PPI efforts. To test the possibility that the effects kicked in before or after SY 2012–2013, we ran the analyses assuming the first treatment year was SY 2009–2010, SY 2010–2011, etc. We did this both for the analysis that considers only schools with newly placed principals to be treated and for the analysis that considers all schools to be treated. In both cases, there was some evidence of the estimated treatment effects increasing starting around SY 2012–2013—the time when implementation of the PPI became clearly visible across districts.

Alternative Approach Estimating the PPI Effect for Newly Placed Principals from the Time They Arrive

Our approach to estimating the effect of the PPI on schools that receive a newly placed principal after SY 2011–2012 compared the change in outcomes from a pre-PPI baseline year in 2010–2011. We performed an alternative analysis in which we measured effects relative to the year before a new principal assumes the principalship, whatever year that might have been. In this alternative specification, the comparison year varied depending on the year of new principal placement. We matched schools that received a newly placed principal in PPI districts to comparison schools in non-PPI districts that were similar as of the year before the new principal's placement. While this approach had some advantages, it also had an important downside. For most cohorts of newly placed principals—all but the SY 2012–2013 cohort—that baseline year was within the period of PPI implementation for the PPI district. To the extent that there was a district-wide effect of the PPI, schools in PPI districts had *also* been "treated" by the PPI during the time designated as a baseline in this approach The effect measured would thus fail to include some of the PPI effect because it would be net of any district-wide effect during that period. The analysis we conducted using this alternative approach showed effects that were smaller in magnitude than those found with our main effects analysis but were still statistically significant.

The Findings Were Robust to Other Sensitivity Checks

We tested the sensitivity of our findings to the inclusion of charter schools by performing an analysis where we excluded all charter schools. For the primary analysis, we included charter schools in the three PPI districts where the district had some jurisdiction over or involvement with charter schools within their boundaries; we excluded the charter schools that were located in the other districts. In this sensitivity analysis, we excluded charter schools for all PPI districts. The results were very close to those found in the primary analysis—different by an average of less than one-tenth of a percentile point. This is primarily driven by the fact that the districts that have jurisdiction over charter schools do not have many charter schools, proportionally.

We also performed an analysis in which we dropped all schools that were newly opened and thus lacked some or all baseline data. Here again, the estimated treatment effects were very similar to those found in the primary analysis, which includes these schools.

Exploratory Analyses

Having examined the effects of the PPI overall and the results of sensitivity analysis, we now turn to more exploratory analysis. These exploratory analyses address questions of interest where data availability or the nature of PPI implementation limited our ability to conduct rigorous analysis. While these analyses provide some tentative insights about interesting topics, they are grouped together here because they must be interpreted more cautiously than the causal analyses in earlier sections of this chapter. The results provide clues about how the PPI played out and may suggest directions for future research but do not provide clear evidence.

We used these analyses to explore the relationship between the PPI and additional outcomes for which data were available for some but not all states. We also explore how treatment effects varied by school characteristics. Finally, we explore the potential contribution of the different components of the pipeline. Limitations of all these analyses are described in Chapter Two.

The Relationship Between PPI and Other School Outcomes Was Mixed

We examined the relationship between the PPI and the following outcomes: science percentile scores, social studies percentile scores, attendance rate, graduation rate, non-suspension rate, non-expulsion rate, participation in career and technical education (CTE), percentage of teachers with certifications, teacher diploma rate, principal and teacher climate ratings, principal's rating of overall school climate, and teacher retention metrics. Whereas for mathematics and reading achievement and principal retention we had data for all PPI districts, for other outcomes, data were available for only some of the PPI districts. Because of this limitation, we describe the findings with a broad brush here and in Tables 4.1 and 4.2. More detail appears in Appendix D: Each outcome we studied is defined in Table D.2, and each aggregate estimate of effect is presented in Table D.3.

We describe treatment effects as favorable if the outcome for treated schools was different in a way that is generally considered to reflect better performance (e.g., higher rates of attendance or higher school climate ratings). We describe treatment effects as negative if the outcome for treated schools was different in a way that is generally considered to suggest worse performance (e.g., lower teacher climate rating or higher expulsion rate). We categorized findings related to teacher turnover as ambiguous because we do not have the kind of teacher-quality data that would allow us to say whether higher turnover is positive or negative. We also categorized findings related to student participation in CTE as ambiguous for a similar reason.

We found evidence that the PPI had a favorable effect (in PPI districts where the relevant data are available) on the percentage of teachers with required certifications, on science achievement, on social studies achievement, and on the principal's rating of overall school climate by the second and the third or later years after a school gets a newly placed principal. We found evidence that the PPI had an unfavorable effect on teacher ratings of school climate two years after a school gets a newly placed prin-

Table 4.1
Average Treatment Effects for All Tested Outcomes, Second Year After Placement

	Statistically Significant at the 5% Level	Statistically Insignificant at the 5% Level
Positive effect of the PPI	• Percentage of teachers with certifications • Principal's rating of overall school climate • Science percentile scores • Social studies percentile scores	• Attendance rate • Climate rating • Graduation rate • Non-suspension rate • Teacher diploma rate
Negative effect of the PPI	• Teacher's average climate rating • Teacher's rating of overall school climate	• Non-expulsion rate • Teacher's rating of overall school climate
Ambiguous		• Higher teacher 1-year retention • Lower retention for teachers with fewer than five years of experience • Lower student CTE participation rate

Table 4.2
Average Treatment Effects for All Tested Outcomes, Third and Later Years After Placement

	Statistically Significant at 5% Level	Statistically Insignificant at 5% Level
Positive effect of the PPI	• Percentage of teachers with certifications • Social studies percentile scores • Principal's average climate rating	• Attendance rate • Climate rating • Graduation rate • Non-expulsion rate • Principal's rating of overall school climate • Science percentile scores • Teacher's average climate rating • Teacher's rating of overall school climate
Negative effect of the PPI		• Non-suspension rate • Teacher diploma rate
Ambiguous	• Lower teacher retention • Lower teacher retention for teachers with fewer than five years of experience • Higher teacher 1-year retention	• Lower student CTE participation rate

cipal, but that unfavorable effect is no longer present three or more years after getting a newly placed principal. We found that the PPI is associated with higher rates of teacher turnover for teachers with fewer than five years of experience but lower rates of overall teacher turnover three or more years after the placement of a new principal. Attendance and graduation outcomes reflect favorably on the PPI, although the relationships are not statistically significant. These effects are summarized in Tables 4.1 and 4.2. Because this analysis was exploratory in nature, we made no corrections for multiple hypotheses.

Effects of the PPI May Be Smaller for Schools with Relatively Fewer White and Affluent Students

To examine whether PPI effects are stronger or weaker for schools serving different student populations, we conducted an exploratory regression analysis relating effect size to school characteristics. Looking at student demographics, we found that within the PPI districts—which serve predominantly high-needs student populations—the PPI effects tended to be smaller in schools serving lower proportions of white students or higher proportions of students eligible for free and reduced-price lunch.

These findings are consistent with findings from subgroup analyses focused on schools serving high proportions of non-white students (more than 50 percent and more than 75 percent non-white), as well as analyses of schools serving a high proportion of students eligible for free and reduced-price lunch, as reported in Figures D.9 and D.10. These subgroup analyses suggest that schools in PPI districts that served more-disadvantaged student populations had smaller, but still positive, effects compared with schools in PPI districts that served less-disadvantaged student populations. However, the differences across these subgroups were not statistically significant.

Other Descriptive Outcomes

Four PPI districts provided principal evaluation data for all principals. In these districts, we examined evaluation ratings for newly placed principals relative to the district as a whole. First, and as we would expect, we found that, in all four of these districts, evaluation scores for new principals were lower than for more-experienced principals. Second, we found that principals who transfer from one school to another tended to have below-average evaluation scores in the year prior to their transfer and improved, though still below average, evaluation scores in the year after their transfer. This suggests that, in several PPI districts, principals who were underperforming were likely to transfer, and that after transferring they performed somewhat better. This apparent improvement in the match between principal and school after a transfer may or may not relate to the strategic reforms implemented by PPI districts.

We also conducted an exploratory analysis of the evaluation ratings of principals who left the PPI districts (see Text Box 4.1) and found that their ratings were substantially below the district average during the period of the study. This suggests that the PPI districts may have been using evaluation data to inform decisions about veteran principals.

Text Box 4.1. Departing Principals

As part of the PPI and at varying points in time during the study period, each district adopted new principal evaluation systems. Data from these systems provide some descriptive insights about principals who left their district during the period of the study. Across the five PPI districts from which we were able to obtain evaluation scores from all school principals, principals who left PPI districts between SYs 2011–2012 and 2016–2017 were rated as below average in every case. On average, departing principal evaluation ratings were 0.44 standard deviations below the mean, with individual district-level averages for departing principals ranging from 0.15 to 0.80 standard deviations below the mean.

Unfortunately, we lack sufficient data to conduct a robust analysis of trends in the quality of principals who left the PPI districts. It may be typical for departing principals to be lower-performing than principals who remain in their districts, and we lack comparative data to explore how similar PPI districts are to other districts in this respect. The only certain conclusion from our data is that none of the PPI districts were, on average, losing principals that they considered to be higher-performing during the period after they implemented reforms to their comprehensive principal evaluation systems.

We Found Little Evidence That Individual Pipeline Components Had a Larger (or Smaller) Contribution to Effects Than Other Components

We investigated the possibility that specific pipeline components were driving the observed effects on achievement and principal retention by examining whether exposure to individual pipeline components influenced these effects. Although answers to this question could potentially help districts know what to emphasize, in fact the findings are much too equivocal to support advice of this kind. The school-level multivariate and univariate models used in this analysis, as described in Chapter Two and Appendix D, were subject to challenges that stem from the nature of PPI implementation. Thus, the findings shown in Tables D.4 and D.5 in Appendix D should be viewed as highly exploratory in nature. They may warrant further investigation in other research, however, and therefore are briefly summarized here.

We found that higher prescreening "talent pool" scores for newly hired principals were associated with significantly larger effects on achievement outcomes. This suggests that the screening ratings districts created may have been successful in differentiating between principals who were more or less likely to be effective school leaders.[3]

In a set of analyses in which we examined relationships between PPI effects and components without controlling for exposure to other components (the univariate regressions), we found some evidence that PPI effects are larger after the adoption of leader standards and new evaluation systems. These analyses suffer from limitations, because exposure to these components does not vary for a given cohort of newly placed principals in a district, and some districts had already implemented these features prior to the launch of the PPI.

We found some evidence that exposure to a residency-based preservice program is associated with smaller PPI effects. This is observed in both the univariate analysis and in the analysis that controlled for other factors for new district hires. However, we caution readers against drawing conclusions about the effectiveness of residency-based programs, because this correlation was driven by data from one of the six PPI districts. We do not observe what led districts to hire from residency or nonresidency programs, and this correlation does not necessarily indicate that residency training was detrimental to performance.

Finally, we observed a correlation between a newly hired principal's exposure to induction-related PD and larger positive retention effects but smaller achievement effects (in both multivariate and univariate analyses). This suggests that induction-related training may have helped to retain principals in their schools but that these schools did not have better outcomes. However, we do not know whether there is any bias in terms of who was selected to receive PD—for instance, if PD was provided

---

[3]   We cannot observe, however, the extent to which talent pools and selective hiring contributed to screening out the lowest-rated potential hires. This means that talent pool systems may have contributed even more to the PPI effect than this association suggests.

more often to principals who were either more or less likely to remain at their school because of other factors.

Because neither the initiative nor the study was designed to identify the effects of any specific component in isolation from others, it is not possible to causally disentangle the effect of any specific component. These correlational findings should be interpreted with great caution.

Academic Return-on-Investment Findings

Given our estimates for the effects and the cost of the PPI, we found that the initiative is quite cost-effective when it comes to raising student achievement. Because the PPI reforms support school principals, they cost relatively little while benefiting a large number of students per affected principal. Overall across the PPI districts, 56 percent of schools in the PPI districts received a new principal after SY 2011–2012 and were thus counted in our primary analysis as "treated" at some point in the study period. This includes a mix of schools with one year, two years, and three or more years of exposure to PPI-related reforms. We estimate that the exposure-weighted average PPI effect size in mathematics over all of these schools was 2.65 percentile point gains on state tests, while the weighted average effect size in reading was 5.51 percentile point gains. The total cost of PPI-related reforms over the five-year period was $210 per student present in the district during that period,[4] but when we conservatively focus solely on benefits to students in "treated" schools (i.e., those in schools with newly placed principals), while maintaining this full cost spread across whole districts, the per-treated-student cost comes to $373 per student. This means that for every $100 spent per student over five years on PPI-related reforms, we estimate that student achievement increased by around 1.5 percentile points in reading and about two-thirds of a percentile point in mathematics.

The prior estimate includes all the costs of the PPI but does not include benefits to students in schools that do not receive a new principal during this period. If instead we estimate benefits for all students based on our effect estimates for the impacts of the PPI on the districts as a whole, we estimate an even more efficient ROI of approximately 2.4 percentile points in reading and 1 percentile point in mathematics for each $100 spent per student over five years.[5] Given that total average annual per pupil expenditures in PPI districts ranged from $8,198 to $17,297 during the PPI depending

---

[4]   Per-student cost is based on the costs per year and the number of students present in each year of the study. Consequently, the five-year cost per student counts five years of per student annual costs, even though the sample of individual students present each year in the district changes over time.

[5]   Treatment effects on all schools use our 3+-year estimates for effects on all schools (2.29 percentile points in mathematics and 5.01 percentile points in reading), because over the five-year period of the study virtually all schools in each district had at least three years of exposure to the PPI reforms. Further, our costs are no longer

on the district and year (Kaufman, Gates, et al., 2017, pp. 30–31), these expenditures are quite modest. In addition, the above estimates assume that there are no benefits to PPI-related practices that would linger if funding of those practices ceased after the five-year window that we observe. This is likely a conservative assumption.

Studies that include both cost estimates and comparable outcome measures for students are not yet common in K–12 education research. We were able to identify two points of comparison from research on other educational interventions in similar contexts and using similar outcomes. However, we caution readers that these interventions involved short-term exposure to a narrowly targeted intervention, with outcomes measured in the same year. Measured benefits of these interventions to students should, however, still be comparable, even if PPI effects are measured after more than one year. First, Kim et al. (2016) measured the costs and effects of a low-cost, large-scale summer reading intervention. They estimated per-student costs ($250–$480) that were similar to the PPI costs ($200 district-wide or $373 counting just "treated" schools), with effect sizes in reading less than one-quarter as large as we observe for the PPI in reading. Second, Jacob, Armstrong, and Willard (2015) measured the costs and effects of a volunteer tutoring program in underresourced elementary schools. They estimated a per-student annual cost ($710) to schools that was substantially higher than the PPI costs, with comparable effect sizes in reading relative to the PPI effects in reading. Overall, the PPI reforms appear to have had a meaningful benefit to students at comparatively low cost to districts.

Summary

Implementation of the PPI had positive effects on achievement in reading and mathematics over a two- and three-year period. These statistically significant effects are evident in schools that received a newly placed principal after the start of PPI-supported activities, and lesser but still noteworthy effects are evident in schools district-wide. Additionally, principals who were newly placed during the PPI stayed in their schools longer than principals in similar comparison schools in non-PPI districts. These are the main effects investigated in this evaluation. Sensitivity checks indicate that they hold under different approaches that we tested. Other findings reported in this chapter are based on additional subgroup and exploratory analyses that lend some corroboration to the main findings and suggest areas for further study.

Findings that tend to corroborate the main findings are the prevalence of positive effects on achievement across districts and grade levels, and the more-positive effects found in schools that had new principal hires (who had, overall, greater exposure to

---

diluted as they were in the "treated" school ROI estimate. The combination of factors boosts the effective ROI substantially.

the PPI components than principals reassigned from other principalships in the same district). These subgroup analyses support the inference that the PPI worked as it was intended to work.

The subgroup analysis by prior achievement suggests that the PPI districts had success in their efforts to improve their lowest-achieving schools by placing and supporting strong principals. At the same time, the exploratory analysis of effects in relation to student demographics suggests that schools with the highest proportions of students of color or students living in poverty, although showing positive effects under the PPI, may have needed still more concerted attention to close the achievement gap.

Overall, the findings of this study show that the PPI is a notably effective initiative, particularly in comparison with the relatively few other initiatives that have sought to improve achievement at scale through levers available to district managers. It is also cost-effective. We elaborate in the next chapter, which draws conclusions and implications.

CHAPTER FIVE

Discussion and Recommendations

Districts matter in shaping school leadership. The work they do to manage principals—the pipeline activities—is important. Our study provides compelling evidence that if districts approach these pipeline activities strategically, paying attention to each component and the coherence of the efforts, they set up their newly placed principals for success. The study suggests that this work is feasible, affordable, and effective. Principal pipelines appear to have tangible benefits for districts, schools, school leaders, and students. Student outcomes are better, and newly placed principals are more likely to stay in their jobs.

Our key findings are summarized in Text Box 5.1 and discussed below.

The Work Is Feasible: All Six PPI Districts Were Able to Implement Comprehensive Pipelines, and They Did So in Different Ways

It is feasible for committed districts to do this work. All six large urban districts, selected for the PPI based in part on their existing commitment to school leadership as a school improvement strategy, made further progress during the PPI to improve the way they were carrying out pipeline activities. They all had different starting points, faced different opportunities and constraints, and went about the work in different ways. All of the districts made improvements to their pipeline activities. At the start of the initiative, three of the districts already had implemented the intended systems corresponding to one or more PPI components. The other three districts had more room to grow during the PPI because they had not fully implemented the intended systems corresponding to any of the PPI components.

By SY 2016–2017, all six PPI districts had implemented the full range of activities related to the management of school leaders (see Text Box 3.1), purposefully choosing to engage or not engage in specific activities. All of the districts had adopted leader standards and were using those standards to inform other components of the pipeline. They had all developed LTSs. They were engaging in strategic hiring and placement for principals, using data from LTSs and practical demonstrations of competencies in the hiring process. Each district had a district-run principal preparation program for its

Text Box 5.1. Summary of Key Findings

The work is feasible.

- PPI districts were able to implement all components of a principal pipeline at scale.
- PPI districts approached pipeline enhancement in different ways depending on their starting point, needs, and opportunities.

The work is effective.

- After three or more years, schools with newly placed principals in PPI districts outperformed comparison schools with newly placed principals by 6.22 percentile points in reading and 2.87 percentile points in math. These statistically significant and meaningful effects imply that a school that received a new principal and whose students would otherwise have been at the median in reading achievement would have scored above the 56th percentile as a result of the PPI. We refer to this as the *main PPI effect* on achievement outcomes.
- Newly placed principals in PPI districts were 5.8 percentage points more likely to remain in their school for two years and 7.8 percentage points more likely to remain in their school for three years than newly placed principals in comparison schools. These statistically significant and meaningful effects imply that for every 100 newly placed principals, the PPI is associated with nearly six fewer losses after two years and nearly eight fewer losses after three years.
- We found statistically significant, positive effects of the PPI on achievement in elementary and middle schools and some evidence of positive effects for high schools.
- PPI effects on achievement were positive and statistically significant for schools in the lowest quartile of the achievement distribution and larger than for schools in the second-lowest quartile.
- PPI effects were positive and statistically significant in reading for five PPI districts and in mathematics in three districts. The PPI effect was negative and statistically significant in mathematics in one district.
- The three PPI districts that had the most room to grow on all components of the pipeline at the start of the study had positive PPI effects on achievement.
- Across PPI districts, novice principals' ratings of their hiring, evaluation, and support experiences improved meaningfully between 2013 and 2015.

The work is affordable.

- PPI districts spent about $42 per student per year on pipeline activities during the initiative. The lowest-cost components were the development of leader standards and selective hiring and placement.
- The per-student costs of the PPI are small relative to the student achievement benefits, based on a comparison between the academic return on investment (ROI) for PPI and other educational interventions.

What drove these effects?

- The entire package of PPI components appears to have worked as a cohesive whole, much as it was designed to do. We found little evidence that individual components were uniquely correlated with larger or smaller effect sizes.

high-potential APs and a partnership of some kind with one or more external programs of principal preparation. Each district continued to provide mentoring for novice principals and had a principal evaluation system that used the district's leader standards.

While these similarities are real, the districts had important flexibility to approach the pipeline activities in ways that made sense given their contexts and to adjust their strategies over time. PPI districts allocated resources across pipeline activities differently. Some put a greater emphasis on preservice preparation than others. Some devoted more resources to on-the-job support than others. Moreover, the districts adopted different approaches to providing preservice and on-the-job support. For example, in crafting strategies related to induction support, some districts concentrated the support in the first year, and others spread it out over four or five years. Because there was so much variation in how PPI districts accomplished the work, their experience does not provide a specific recipe for other districts.

The Work Is Affordable: The Efforts of PPI Districts to Operate and Enhance Their Pipelines Cost Less Than 0.5 Percent of District Budgets

It cost PPI districts about $42 per pupil per year, or less than 0.5 percent of the district's budget in each school year, to operate and enhance principal pipelines. This estimate includes the cost of any pipeline activities that may have been fully or partially in place prior to the launch of the PPI—activities such as operation of the Quality-Plus Leader Academy in Gwinnett County or operation of the talent pool in Charlotte-Mecklenburg. For comparison, the resources that these districts devoted to the PPI are roughly one-quarter of the resources districts in the Partnerships for Effective Teaching initiative devoted to that work, which centered on strengthening systems of teacher evaluation. According to Stecher et al. (2018), the three school districts that implemented the Partnerships for Effective Teaching initiative spent between $265 and $590 per pupil, amounting to between 2.12 and 2.97 percent of the district budget, in SY 2015–2016 (pp. 344–345).

Some of the pipeline work done by districts during the PPI, and accounted for by these cost figures, was devoted to functions that they would have been carrying out anyway—hiring, evaluation, and support. We estimated that pipeline expenditures by PPI districts in the year before the launch of the initiative (SY 2010–2011) were at least half (and possibly more) of what the expenditures were in the first year of the initiative. Supporting the PPI involved a broad-based commitment on the part of a school district to have district staff dedicate their time to this work. Nearly half of the PPI expenditures (44 percent) were due to costs of district personnel time devoted to the initiative. The commitment was not just to doing new things but to doing routine things in new ways.

We estimated that, for every $100 spent per student over five years on PPI-related reforms, student achievement increased by between 1 and 2.4 percentile points in reading and about one-third of a percentile point to 1 percentile point in mathematics.

The Work Is Effective: Our Analysis Suggests That the PPI Benefited Schools

Our main analysis found positive effects of the PPI on a wide range of outcomes that school districts care about. Evidence of such positive effects was variable but remarkably pervasive across outcomes we looked at, across districts, and across school grade spans.

First and foremost, we found evidence of positive effects on both mathematics and reading achievement in PPI districts. Specifically, schools in PPI districts that receive a new principal outperform comparison schools by 4.94 percentile points in reading and 2.61 percentile points in mathematics after two years—findings that are statistically significant at the 1-percent level. After three or more years, treated schools outperform comparison schools by 6.22 percentile points in reading and 2.87 percentile points in math, again statistically significant. Effects are larger for the third year for both subjects, and the effects are larger for reading than for mathematics. The results for reading are of a magnitude that is sizable—over a 6-percentile-point increase.

Putting this another way, our results suggest that a school that received a new principal and whose students would have otherwise been at the median (50th percentile) in reading achievement without the PPI instead would have reading achievement scores above the 56th percentile as a result of the PPI. We found no other district-wide initiatives with demonstrated effects of this magnitude on achievement. Some charter school interventions, as well as some school- and classroom-level interventions, have demonstrated similar or larger effects, but for more-targeted populations. For example, Tuttle et al. (2015) looked at the outcomes of students in 43 KIPP middle schools and found that mathematics and English language arts achievement gains of KIPP students were 7 and 6 percentile points greater, respectively, than for comparison students. Clark et al. (2013) found that students in grades 6–12 who were in classrooms taught by Teach for America members experienced mathematics achievement gains that were 3 percentile points higher than students in comparison classrooms. Cowan and Goldhaber (2016) identified smaller effects of exposure to a teacher who meets National Board for Professional Teaching Standards on mathematics and reading achievement (on the order of 1 to 2 percentile points) among elementary and middle school students in Washington state.

The PPI Benefited All Schools, Not Just Those That Received a Newly Placed Principal

We also found evidence of positive, but somewhat smaller, district-wide effects of the PPI on both mathematics and reading achievement in PPI districts, using a different approach that considers effects on all schools as of a certain point in time. Schools in PPI districts overall outperformed comparison schools by 5.01 percentile points in reading and 2.29 percentile points in mathematics three or more years after SY 2012–2013—findings that are statistically significant at the 1-percent level.

At first glance, this is a puzzling finding. The initial rationale for launching the PPI was framed in terms of bringing strong new candidates into the principalship and effectively deploying and supporting them. Designers of the initiative did not envision that it would make a difference in all schools, including those where veteran principals stayed in place. Yet our two sets of findings—effects on schools with newly placed principals and on all schools in PPI districts—imply that the PPI benefited not only schools that received a newly placed principal, but all schools in the district.

How could this have happened? One or more or the following factors may be contributing to the district-wide finding. First, among the pipeline reforms encouraged in the PPI are several reforms—leader standards development, changes to principal evaluation, enhanced principal supervision and support—that could affect all sitting principals, potentially leading to improvements in performance of veteran principals and newly placed principals (e.g., by providing targeted support to struggling veteran principals). Second, because The Wallace Foundation selected districts for participation in the PPI partly on the basis of their prior experience with pipeline reforms, these efforts were already underway prior to the launch of the PPI. These activities could very well have benefited some of the principals who were already in place before 2012–2013. A third factor, related to the first two, is that pipeline reforms may have enhanced the candidate pool to the point where PPI districts could confidently remove veteran principals who were underperforming and not improving in spite of additional supports. As discussed in Text Box 4.1, we observe that evaluation ratings of principals who left the PPI districts were substantially below the district average during the period of the study. Their departure could also have contributed to improvements in principals' performance on average.

All three of these possible explanations are consistent with the design of the initiative and with the inference that the PPI worked as hoped. A fourth possible explanation is different: The PPI districts may have initiated other district-wide reform activities that were unrelated to the pipeline, but that coincidentally contributed to improvements in principal performance during the period of the grant and study. It is true that each of the states and/or districts had other initiatives that overlapped in time with the PPI. However, there were no other initiatives that these districts had in common that were substantial and did not also affect comparison districts in the state. One major initiative that did overlap with the PPI in one of the participating districts was unlikely to have contributed positively to the findings presented in this report. Still, any of the four explanations for the district-wide effects could be true. Indeed, several could be true at the same time.

Our findings further indicate that principal pipelines had a favorable effect on the retention of newly placed principals. Newly placed principals in PPI districts were 5.8 percentage points more likely than comparison principals to remain in their school for two years and 7.8 percentage points more likely to remain in their school for three years compared with newly placed principals in similar schools in non-PPI districts. That means that for every 100 newly placed principals, PPI districts had nearly six fewer losses after two years and nearly eight fewer losses after three years

We also found suggestive evidence that the PPI had a favorable effect in schools that received a newly placed principal on the percentage of teachers with required certifications, science achievement, social studies achievement, and teacher one-year retention rates by the third or later years after the arrival of a new principal.

Positive Effects of the PPI Appear to Be Widespread

We found positive effects of the PPI across a variety of subgroups defined in terms of districts, grade spans, and prior principal experience in the district. The pattern of effects we observed lends further support for the inference that the PPI was a benefit to districts.

When we looked at the effects on achievement by district, we found that effects were mostly positive. The PPI effects on reading achievement were positive and statistically significant in five of six districts, and the effects on mathematics achievement were positive and statistically significant in three districts. In one district, the PPI effect on mathematics achievement was negative and statistically significant. In that district, the negative results were concentrated in elementary schools. This suggests that while positive PPI effects were widespread, they were not guaranteed. We did find that the three districts that had the most room to grow during the PPI because they had not fully implemented the intended systems corresponding to any of the PPI components prior to the PPI all had positive outcomes that are statistically significant in one or both subjects. Retention effects by district were more varied. This variation could reflect differences in the districts' starting points with regard to the depth of the candidate pool, local context factors influencing the labor market for principals, or district approaches to principal reassignment at the start of the initiative.

We found statistically significant positive PPI effects on mathematics achievement for elementary, middle, and high schools and on reading for elementary and middle schools. The broad span of positive effects across these school types is encouraging in view of the challenges that many districts face with staffing administrative positions in middle and high schools.

Our subgroup analysis focused on the subset of newly placed principals who were new principal hires is more exploratory in nature, because we cannot distinguish between new principal hires and reassigned principals in comparison districts. However, that analysis provides suggestive evidence that average treatment effects across districts for new principal hires, who are the target of pipeline efforts, are larger than for reassigned principals, particularly for mathematics achievement and for retention.

PPI Effects Kicked in Early

Our analysis also provides evidence that the PPI benefits kicked in quickly and were evident for the earliest cohorts of PPI principals—possibly reflecting effects of activities that districts undertook prior to the formal launch of the PPI. Effects on achievement appear to be stable over time for new district hires, and effects on principal retention appear to be increasing over time. This is consistent with the general pattern of PPI implementation, year by year. These districts had prior efforts related to the pipeline activities and thus had many of the features in place prior to the launch of the initiative. They made early investments in induction support for novice principals. They then expanded that support while beefing up hiring processes. Moreover, the growth in retention effects over time could indicate that efforts to improve preservice preparation have begun to enhance the quality of the candidate pool or that district efforts in hiring and placement or on-the-job support are improving over time.

Effects of the PPI on Achievement Are Larger for Schools in the Lowest Quartile of the Achievement Distribution but Possibly Smaller for Schools Serving More Students of Color and More Students in Poverty

We found evidence of larger positive effects of the PPI for schools in the lowest quartile of the achievement distribution (prior to the PPI) compared with schools in the second-lowest quartile for both subjects. Positive effects in this lowest quartile were larger than those for the top quartile in reading, and not smaller than any other quartile. This suggests that the lowest-performing schools in PPI districts benefited in meaningful ways from improvements in school leadership.

On the other hand, analyses by demographics within the school show weaker—though still positive and statistically significant—effects in schools serving high proportions of students of color or students eligible for free or reduced-price lunch. Like all of our exploratory findings, these should be viewed with caution. But because equity for student populations disadvantaged as a result of their race or poverty is an important policy concern for the local, state, and national levels, these results may warrant attention in practice and research. Future initiatives in principal leadership could be crafted with an eye to improving leadership for schools with high proportions of students of color or students living in poverty, and they could be studied with designs well suited to assessing and understanding their effects for such students.

PPI Components Appear to Work as a Cohesive Whole

Our analysis is consistent with the theory that comprehensive efforts to strategically implement pipeline activities across all components and align them with leader standards—which all districts did—are what matter. The component-by-component analysis found limited evidence that any one component or aspect of the pipeline efforts was associated with effects. This should not be interpreted to mean that any one component can be ignored.

Because neither the initiative nor the study was designed to identify the effects of any specific component in isolation from others, we are unable to causally disentangle the effect of any specific component, and the handful of correlations we identified should be interpreted with great caution. We discuss them because they raise interesting questions about the details of pipeline implementation that are worthy of further investigation. For example, we identified a negative correlation between an individual principal's participation in a preservice program that included a residency-based experience and achievement effects for that principal's school. Although this correlation appears to be driven by results from one district, it is a subject worthy of further investigation, in part because there is a research base suggesting such program features are effective. Similarly, we saw a correlation between newly hired principals' exposure to induction-related PD and positive retention effects but negative effects on student achievement. More research is needed to understand how induction supports are targeted and their effectiveness.

Caveats and Limitations

The nature of the PPI as an initiative or intervention posed challenges for evaluating the effects of PPI-related activities. Our main analysis of effects focused on newly placed principals and the schools they lead, comparing outcomes for these principals and schools with outcomes of newly placed principals in other districts that did not implement the PPI. We focused our attention on SY 2012–2013 as the first year when newly placed principals were considered treated. Because the PPI represented a set of guidelines rather than a specific design, PPI districts did different things at different times. All districts continued to modify their pipeline activities throughout the initiative and beyond. This means that there is no bright line that districts crossed allowing for a clear distinction between pre-PPI and PPI conditions. In this report, we are transparent about the choices we have made in this evaluation. In preparing this report, we did numerous sensitivity checks, which suggest that our choices and assumptions were conservative—meaning that if we had made different choices, the findings we emphasize would be similar but even stronger.

Because the PPI was a district-wide intervention, a chief criticism is likely to be that the effects we observe are due to other things going on in the districts, and not the PPI. This concern may be amplified by the finding that PPI effects appear to hold across all schools, not just those that receive a newly placed principal. But, as discussed above, the PPI could have had a district-wide effect for several reasons. The notion that unrelated activities alone caused the observed effect across all the districts seems less plausible.

Recommendations for Districts

This study provides encouraging evidence that school districts can move the needle on student achievement, the retention of newly placed principals, and other outcomes through strategic and coherent principal pipeline activities.

Our overarching recommendation is that districts should think strategically about the full range of pipeline activities and make smart investments that account for their local challenges and opportunities. Some specific recommendations follow from consideration of pipeline features or implementation features that were found across all PPI districts. Some of these recommendations for achieving that aim echo recommendations from the final implementation report (Turnbull, Anderson, et al., 2016, pp. 59–62).

Secure Commitment for This Work at the Highest Levels of the District

Principal pipeline activities required engagement from across the districts. For this reason, the work is not likely to move forward or be sustained unless the superintendent and school board are behind it. A substantial share of the costs incurred by the PPI districts were costs associated with the district personnel time. Practically speaking, redirecting some of the work of busy people requires commitment at the highest levels of the district.

Prioritize Leader Standards Efforts

While our study provides evidence that principal pipelines are a lever for school improvement, it does not provide a simple recipe for following in the footsteps of PPI districts. But because the initiative emphasized standards-aligned reforms and the development or adoption of leader standards was inexpensive, a focus on leader standards could be a cost-effective first step for districts. Our study found that all PPI districts adopted leader standards and used those standards to inform other pipeline activities. For example, all PPI districts implemented a standards-based evaluation system during the PPI. They also worked to ground principal job descriptions, hiring criteria, preservice preparation, and on-the-job support in their standards. PPI districts described their leader standards efforts as quick wins because standards supported a strategic approach to pipeline activities and promoted coherence. Because some districts already had standards at the start of the initiative and others rolled them out district-wide early in the initiative, our analysis cannot definitively say that leader standards are more important than any other component of the pipeline. But given that they are the cheapest component to implement, districts looking to begin this work would be wise to begin with efforts to specify leader standards in a way that could give coherence to other pipeline activities.

Identify and Use Data That Can Inform Pipeline Efforts

All six PPI districts developed LTSs, and by the end of the initiative were using those systems to inform strategic hiring and placement. They credited the LTSs with moving key pipeline activities from subjective processes based on "who you know" to objective processes based on demonstrated competencies, experiences, and their relationship to school needs. Districts reported that LTSs allowed them to make better matches between candidates and schools—which could be contributing to stronger retention effects for later cohorts of newly placed principals. Districts can learn from this experience and begin to identify existing or potential sources of data in their own systems.

Commit to the Long Haul

The six PPI districts had already made progress implementing pipeline components prior to the launch of the initiative. They spent five years during the PPI enhancing pipeline activities in their districts. By the end of this study, they still viewed their work as ongoing. Our analysis suggests that the work done by PPI districts prior to the launch of the PPI was already having an effect prior to or early into the PPI implementation phase. And while our findings indicate that the work paid off, there is strong reason to suspect that there are benefits that have not yet been realized. Other districts embarking on these efforts should have realistic expectations about how quickly they might realize effects from their own efforts.

Monitor Performance to Identify Lessons Learned and Tailor Supports

Our finding that PPI effects were larger in the lowest-performing schools suggests that principal pipelines may have helped districts target resources and support to schools serving the lowest-performing students. These finding are encouraging, but also point to the work yet to be done to ensure high-quality leadership across the districts. Schools in the second-lowest quartile of the state achievement distribution are a majority of schools in PPI districts. Lessons from districts' successes in improving the lowest-performing schools may be used to assist schools in the second quartile facing leadership transitions. Districts may be able to use information from LTSs over time to identify the characteristics of principals who succeed in different types of schools and effectively prepare individuals for and support them in these roles. More research into the long-term effect of pipeline efforts for high-needs schools is warranted.

Recommendations for States

The lessons from the work are most clearly relevant to districts, which are responsible for the pipeline activities. However, state leaders interested in supporting school leadership could consider ways in which state action or policy could support districts in pipeline enhancement. In particular, states should consider ways in which state efforts would support principal pipelines in smaller districts that lack the infrastructure to undertake major efforts on their own.

State Leader Standards
State leader standards can provide a useful starting point for district efforts to develop clear, actionable leader standards. Several of the PPI districts were able to leverage state leader standards in developing their own district standards and/or evaluation systems linked to those standards. States should consider whether their leader standards are modern, operational, and relevant to school districts in their state. If not, an effort to revise state leader standards so they can inform pipeline activities at the district level could benefit districts across the state.

Data Systems on School Leaders
School districts tend to be data-rich but information-poor. All PPI districts developed LTSs, which they used to support strategic hiring and placement, vacancy projections, and succession planning. Smaller districts are unlikely to be able to invest in district-specific systems. But states could have a role to play in developing systems that could be leveraged by many districts.

Create Information Sharing Opportunities
PPI districts learned a lot from one another. States could support opportunities for district leaders to share information about challenges and successes related to pipeline activities. In the process, states could learn about state policies that support or inhibit pipeline improvement efforts.

Recommendations for Further Knowledge Building

The six PPI districts demonstrated that it is feasible to implement principal pipelines in large urban districts, but their work is not done, and the effects of their work to date may not be fully realized. It will be important to continue to monitor and learn from the efforts in these districts and other districts that embark on similar work.

Our evaluation was unable to answer some important questions and raised some new ones along the way. We highlight a few areas that seem most worthy of investment in further knowledge building.

How Can Districts and States Support Slightly Underperforming Schools and Their Principals?

Our finding that PPI effects were concentrated in the lowest-performing schools and schools that were above the state average in terms of test scores suggest a need for a more nuanced understanding of how districts can support school leaders in different contexts. With information from LTSs in hand, districts should work to refine their understanding of the relationship between leadership characteristics and school needs, and use that information to inform placement decisions and tailor support.

What Are the Benefits of Research-Based Preservice Preparation, and How Can Districts Ensure Clinical Experiences in a Cost-Effective Manner?

Research on effective principal preparation programs offers a number of suggestions, one of which is that extended supervised internships allow participants to engage in the real work of a school leader and get feedback on their performance (Darling-Hammond et al., 2007). Some have further advocated for the importance of a residency-based experience, where a candidate is placed in a new setting to work for a time under the guidance of a mentor principal (New York City Leadership Academy and American Institutes for Research, 2016). This study found no evidence that residency-based preservice programs provided added benefits in the context of PPI districts that were already working with preferred preservice partners. Since residency-based preservice programs are associated with higher costs, more research is needed to understand cost-effective ways to include clinical learning opportunities in preservice programs.

How Can Districts Design Effective On-the-Job Support?

PPI districts devoted a large share of pipeline resources to on-the-job support. Our analysis suggests that induction mentoring may have been associated with stronger effects. In a context in which districts are acting strategically to deploy pipeline resources effectively, there is much more to be learned about how districts differentiate on-the-job support when they have the information to do so.

Districts looking for ways to enhance school outcomes and improve the retention of newly placed principals should be encouraged by the experiences of PPI districts. Our findings suggest that when districts focused attention on activities related to principal pipelines, principals, schools, and students benefited. The initiative looked different on the ground in different districts, which implies that there is no "recipe" for other districts to follow. Instead, the work involves analyzing conditions, opportunities, and constraints and making strategic choices based on that assessment, and this in turn calls for enduring commitment and an openness to changes in the way districts manage their principal pipeline.

Data

In this chapter, we discuss the sources of the data used in this study. We first discuss data for the PPI districts, and then we discuss the statewide data.

PPI District Data

Districts participating in the PPI provided extensive data about their students, schools, and staff from at least SY 2010–2011 through SY 2016–2017. District-provided data were particularly focused on newly hired or reassigned principals during this study period, with data drawn from LTSs that were implemented as part of the PPI in each district and that captured data about the characteristics, placements, and pipeline-related experiences of individual newly hired school principals.

In addition to data provided by the PPI districts themselves, we were also provided extensive qualitative data summaries by PSA from its data collection on implementation as part of the overall evaluation of the PPI. These data were essential in documenting the timing and nature of district-wide reforms that were adopted as part of the PPI and related to each of the individual PPI components (i.e., leader standards, selection, and hiring). Through in-depth analysis of the implementation of the PPI, as well as extensive survey data of school principals in the PPI districts, PSA was able to provide clear and well-documented descriptions of how the PPI reforms, including each separate component of the PPI, evolved over time in each participating district. While PSA's data indicate how each component of the PPI was implemented in a gradual fashion over time, they also allowed us to identify key inflection points over the period of study when more-substantive reforms were first adopted by districts.

The primary utility of these data was to facilitate our exploratory analyses linking estimated treatment effects at the school level with either the timing of key components of the PPI reforms or with individual school principals' exposure to key components of the PPI reforms.

In particular, as discussed in Appendix E, we were able to categorize the exposure of individual treated schools to the components of the PPI as follows:

- **Leader standards reforms.** As part of the PPI, participating districts redefined and articulated standards for principals' professional practice. Because these reforms were district-wide, exposure to this component of the PPI reforms did not vary on an individual principal basis. Instead, whole districts adopted or made substantial changes to leader standards at particular points in time. The implementation data provided by PSA allowed us to identify the school year in which each individual PPI district made the most-substantial reforms to its leader standards, and we defined the periods before and after these reforms using a binary (0/1) variable for each school district. In our exploratory analyses, we looked for variation in estimated treatment effects across all schools in each district corresponding to the timing of these reforms in that district.

- **Residency-based preservice programs.** The PPI districts focused on improving the quality of the principal preservice training programs that trained new principals entering the principal pipeline. One aspect of preservice programs that was emphasized was in-school residency training, where *residency* is defined as a clinical placement of at least one month in a school other than the one in which the candidate has already been working. Using data provided by the districts' LTSs, we flagged novice principals who graduated from programs with a residency component using a binary (0/1) variable. We note that, in one district, almost all new principals were trained in residency programs, limiting our ability to distinguish the contributions of residency experiences to that district's overall treatment effect estimates.

- **Preferred preservice programs.** The PPI districts designated specific preservice programs as "preferred" if they met specific criteria related to the training provided. However, districts varied in the extent to which graduation from preferred programs was prioritized in principal hiring. In a few districts, all or almost all new hires came from preferred programs, whereas in most districts new hires came from both preferred and non-preferred preservice training programs. Using data provided by the districts' LTSs, we flagged novice principals who graduated from programs that districts labeled as preferred using a binary (0/1) variable. Note that, in almost all cases, residency-based preservice programs were also identified as "preferred" programs as part of the PPI, but not every preferred program had a residency component.

- **Participation in a "talent pool."** PPI districts became more systematic over time in how they screened and kept track of potential new principal hires using "talent pools." Talent pools came into being at different times in different districts, and in many cases not every new principal hire was documented as being a part of a talent pool, even once the talent pool system was established. Using data provided by the districts' LTSs, we flagged novice principals who were documented as part of a talent pool prior to hire using a binary (0/1) variable. We hypothesize that, to some extent, variation in talent pool documentation may reflect imperfect record-keeping by districts, although there are also likely were principals whose route to hiring did not involve a talent pool even after districts had established one.

- **Rating scores from talent pools.** A key purpose of talent pool systems in PPI districts was to document and respond to variation in prescreening evaluations of principal candidates. Five of the six PPI districts provided the individual ratings of newly hired principals using their individual systems for rating potential hires. We standardized talent pool ratings of principals within each district and school year.

- **Evaluation system reforms.** As part of the PPI, participating districts developed and/or reformed their systems for evaluating principals' job performance. Because these reforms were district-wide, exposure to this component of the PPI reforms did not vary on an individual principal basis. Instead, whole districts adopted or made substantial changes to evaluation systems at particular points in time. The implementation data provided by PSA allowed us to gauge the school year in which each individual PPI district made the most-substantial reforms to their evaluation systems, and we defined the period before and after these reforms using a binary (0/1) variable for each school district. In our exploratory analyses, we looked for variation in estimated treatment effects across all schools in each district corresponding to the timing of these reforms in each district.

- **Induction-related professional development.** Districts provided a variety of data regarding the induction-related PD experiences of newly hired principals in their first several years on the job. Some districts provided PD data about all principals (including in some cases additional PD that was not specifically related to induction into a new role), and some districts' PD data included more-specific details about the quantity and types of PD principals engaged in. To create a common indicator of induction-related PD experiences for newly hired principals across the six PPI districts, we created a simple binary flag for each principal indicating whether they received any amount of PD that was specifically labeled as induction-related in their first two years in their new principalship.

- **Induction-related mentoring.**[1] Districts provided a variety of data regarding the mentoring experiences of newly hired principals in their first several years on the job. (Districts varied in whether they used the term *mentoring* or *coaching* for individual support; some had cadres of both mentors and coaches. Because there was no uniform definition of either term across districts, we use *mentoring* for simplicity in this report.) Some districts provided mentoring data about all

---

[1]   In two districts, there was variation in which individual newly hired principals in a district were documented as having received either induction-related PD or mentoring, even when the district policy was that all newly hired principals should receive induction-related PD and/or mentoring. We cannot be sure whether individuals in these circumstances somehow missed or opted out of PD or mentoring experiences, or whether some of the variation in the data may be related to how accurately these experiences were documented. However, we believe that, by and large, the documentation of PD experiences of individual principals was accurate in each district.

principals (including in some cases mentoring that was not specifically related to induction into a new role), and some districts' mentoring data included more-specific details about the quantity and types of mentoring principals engaged in. To create a common indicator of induction-related mentoring experiences for newly hired principals across the six PPI districts, we created a simple binary flag for each principal indicating whether they received any amount of mentoring in their first two years in their new principalship.

State Data

To compare treated schools with similar, untreated schools across their respective states, we collected and cleaned yearly, school-level statewide data for all public schools in each of the six states where the PPI sites under study are located: Colorado, Florida Georgia, Maryland, New York, and North Carolina. We collected data on four sets of variables: new principal appointments (key variable to identify treated schools, and their comparisons), student achievement on mathematics and reading standardized tests (the main outcomes of interest), other school outcomes, and school characteristics for statistical control. We collected these data for each school year in the period between the SY 2006–2007 and the most recently released year of data, generally SY 2016–2017.

We searched and retrieved data from the websites made available by the departments of education of each state, and by the National Center for Education Statistics (NCES). In cases where we did not find publicly downloadable datasets, we submitted formal requests to the appropriate data offices of each state department of education. In two states (Maryland and North Carolina), to obtain the relevant data, RAND signed data safeguarding agreements, establishing data management and storage procedures to protect the confidentiality of individual-level data (such as principal employment records and student test scores and demographics). Table A.1 summarizes the sources of data for each of the six states in the study.

For each state, we cleaned and prepared the raw data for analysis by constructing statewide datasets, with each row representing a unique school-SY observation (with up to ten years of data, or observations, per school), and columns containing the data for each of the variables of interest. We conducted a series of validation tests to ensure that the cleaned data were complete, that their distributions behaved as expected, and that they were consistent with statistics reported at the district and state levels. Finally, we merged cleaned statewide datasets with the PPI treatment indicators, developed with the information provided by each of the six study sites regarding the exposure of new principals to the components of the PPI.

We collected school-level statewide data on the following four sets of variables.

Table A.1
Sources of School-Level, Statewide Data, by State

State	Sources of School-Level, Statewide Data
Colorado	Colorado Department of Education (CDE): • Colorado Education Statistics: http://www.cde.state.co.us/cdereval • CDE Data Lab: http://elm.cde.state.co.us/datalabreport.htm • CDE Assessment Unit: http://www.cde.state.co.us/assessment/ • CDE Data Requests: https://www.cde.state.co.us/cdereval/datarequest
Florida	Florida Department of Education (FLDOE): • PK–12 Public School Data Publications & Reports: http://www.fldoe.org/accountability/data-sys/edu-info-accountability-services/pk-12-public-school-data-pubs-reports/ • K–12 Student Assessment Results: http://www.fldoe.org/accountability/assessments/k-12-student-assessment/results/ • Office of Accountability and Policy Research (PERA Data Requests): http://www.fldoe.org/accountability/accountability-reporting/
Georgia	Georgia Department of Education (GADOE) and Governor's Office of Student Achievement (GOSA): • Free and Reduced-Price Meal Eligibility: https://oraapp.doe.k12.ga.us/ows-bin/owa/fte_pack_frl001_public.entry_form • Criterion-Referenced Competency Tests (CRCT) Statewide Scores: http://www.gadoe.org/Curriculum-Instruction-and-Assessment/Assessment/Pages/CRCT-Statewide-Scores.aspx • End-of-Course Tests (EOCT) Statewide Scores: http://www.gadoe.org/Curriculum-Instruction-and-Assessment/Assessment/Pages/EOCT-Statewide-Scores.aspx • Georgia Milestones Assessment System: http://www.gadoe.org/Curriculum-Instruction-and-Assessment/Assessment/Pages/Georgia-Milestones-Assessment-System.aspx • GADOE Open Records Request: http://www.gadoe.org/Technology-Services/Data-Collections/Pages/Requesting-Data.aspx • High School Cohort Graduation: http://www.gadoe.org/CCRPI/Pages/default.aspx • School Climate: http://www.gadoe.org/External-Affairs-and-Policy/Policy/Pages/School-Climate.aspx • GOSA Downloadable Data: https://gosa.georgia.gov/downloadable-data
Maryland	Maryland State Department of Education (MSDE): • Maryland State Data Downloads: http://reportcard.msde.maryland.gov/ • Datasets that were not publicly available in their website were obtained by request.
New York	New York State Education Department (NYSED): • Office of Information and Reporting Services (IRS), http://www.p12.nysed.gov/irs/ • Downloadable school report cards: https://data.nysed.gov/downloads.php • NYSED Data support Helpdesk (data requests): https://datasupport.nysed.gov/
North Carolina	North Carolina Department of Public Instruction (NCDPI) and NC State Board of Education (SBE): • NC School Report Cards: http://www.ncpublicschools.org/src/researchers/ • North Carolina Education Data Center (NCERDC) (data requests): https://childandfamilypolicy.duke.edu/research/nc-education-data-center/ • Student Accounting: http://www.ncpublicschools.org/fbs/accounting/data/ • Reports and Statistics: http://www.ncpublicschools.org/data/reports/ • Free & Reduced Meals Application Data: http://www.ncpublicschools.org/fbs/resources/data/ • Cohort Graduation Rates: http://www.ncpublicschools.org/accountability/reporting/cohortgradrate • New Teacher Center (school climate surveys, by request): https://ncteachingconditions.org/index
All states	• National Center for Education Statistics (NCES), Elementary and Secondary Information System (ELSI): http://nces.ed.gov/ccd/elsi/

1. New Principal Placements

Treated schools in the study sites were identified as those receiving a new principal once all PPI components were deemed to be in operation in each PPI site (that is, after 2011–2012).[2] To construct a counterfactual, we obtained information on principal turnover in schools across the respective state of each study site. The specific information that was available to identify such changes in school principals varied across states:

- Two states (North Carolina and Maryland) provided detailed longitudinal data on their principal staff, including unique staff identifiers, allowing us to track individual principals across schools and years and to determine when a new principal was appointed in each school. In these cases, the new principal indicator was given the value of 1 in each year in which a new principal ID was observed in any given school (and 0 otherwise).
- Two states (Florida and Colorado) provided lists of schools at which new principals had been placed each year during the period. Schools in these lists were coded 1 in the new principal indicator, and the rest of schools in the state were coded 0.
- Georgia provided lists of schools with the total count of active principals, and the count of principals who "are returning as principals from previous year," per school and school year. The new principal indicator was coded 1 in years when the total count of principals in a school was higher than the count of returning principals, and 0 when both counts were equal.
- New York provided lists with the full names of active principals, by school and year. The new principal indicator was coded 1 for years when the names of principals were first observed in a school, and 0 for years when the names of principals were repeated from any previous years in the same school.

In all cases, the raw data used to construct the new principal indicators were obtained by request to the appropriate data or accountability office, in each state education department. Longitudinal data on principal turnover or new principal appointments in these states were either not publicly available or were publicly available only

---

[2]   A "new principal" can potentially be defined in various ways. In this analysis, we identified a new principal when a person was first appointed as a principal in a school (that is, with the person not having served as principal in that specific school, in previous years). Note that this definition includes both novice principals and veteran principals who are transferred to a new school. This definition was used because it was the only one for which we could construct a consistent indicator measuring new principal appointments, given the data that was available for all six states. Other possible definitions of new principals could not be implemented, given available data; these could have included measuring novice principals (without any previous experience as principals), new principals to-a-district (never before having served in a district), new principals to-a-state (never having served in a state before).

in formats that make data collection costly, and identification of principal turnover prone to errors.[3]

2. Student Test Scores

The main outcome of interest in the study was school-level average student achievement in standardized state tests, primarily focused on mathematics and reading, available in each state. We measured average school achievement in terms of standardized z-scores, by school, year, grade, and subject (setting the mean equal to 0 and the standard deviation equal to 1). The post-regression results were converted to student percentiles. The raw statewide data that we obtained to construct these indicators came in two general forms:

- Two states (North Carolina and Maryland) provided data on individual student-level scores in state tests, in response to our data requests. In these cases, we first calculated school-level score averages by year, grade, and subject, as well as state-level averages and standard deviations (also by year, grade, and subject). We then obtained the school-level z-scores by year, grade, and subject, by subtracting the statewide means and dividing by the statewide standard deviations. Finally, we consolidated z-scores across the different grades into single school-level z-scores by major subject area, as weighted averages of the grade-specific z-scores (using the number of test takers by grade as weights).
- For the other four states (Colorado, Florida, Georgia, and New York), we obtained data on school-level score averages by year, grade, and subject, as well as on statewide test score averages and standard deviations (also by year, grade, and subject). These data were obtained in part from public sources, and in part in response to data requests. Again, we calculated the school-level z-scores by year, by grade, and subject, and then calculated weighted averages across grades and subjects (using number of test takers as weights), in four major subject areas.

3. Other Outcomes

We also obtained and cleaned statewide data on other school-level outcomes, generally published online by the education department of each state:

- **Student attendance rates.** We obtained data on student attendance or absenteeism, as available in each state. Most report the percentage of students attending school every day, while Georgia reports the percentage of students in three catego-

---

[3]   An example of this are the New York State Education Department's yearly directories of school administrators, which are only available in printable PDF format and lack unique identifiers for schools and principals (which are only identified by names, which are sometimes inconsistent across years): http://www.p12.nysed.gov/irs/schoolDirectory/

ries of absenteeism: percentage absent 0 to 5 days, percentage absent 6 to 15 days, and percentage absent more than 15 days.

- **Student expulsion and suspension rates.** We obtained data for all states, though the specific measures vary slightly across states: Some states report short- and long-term rates (North Carolina), whereas others report in-school and out-of-school suspension and/or expulsion rates (Colorado, Florida, Georgia).
- **Four-year high school graduation rates.** For all states, we obtained their reported data on the percentage of high school students who obtain a high school diploma within four years.
- **High school participation rates in career and technical education (CTE) courses.** This was not available for all states. For Colorado, we used the reported percentage of high school students participating in "advanced placement" or "concurrent enrollment" courses.
- **School climate ratings.** These data were obtained only for two states: Georgia and North Carolina.
  - Georgia publishes data on a "School Climate Star Rating," which places schools in one of five categories according to their performance in an index equally weighting four components (each in turn comprising multiple indicators): (1) school climate surveys (teachers, parents, and students), (2) discipline records, (3) safe and substance-free environment, and (4) attendance rates of students and educators.
  - North Carolina provided teacher-level responses to the state's Teacher Working Conditions survey, with their assessments of various school climate domains. We selected and generated school-level averages for items with teacher assessments of their schools as "good place[s] to work and learn," and different aspects of their school's leadership, including problem solving, trust and respect, ease to raise concerns, support to teachers, holding teachers to high professional standards, and effective leadership. These data were obtained by request; school-level results can be retrieved online, but not in dataset form.
- School staff retention or turnover rates.
  - **Principal retention.** For all states, based on the yearly principal turnover data described above, we measured the two- and three-year principal retention rates.
  - **Teacher retention.** For three states (Florida, Georgia, and North Carolina), we obtained one-year teacher turnover or retention rates. For New York, we obtained the turnover rate for all teachers, and the turnover rate of teachers with fewer than five years of experience. Data were not available for Colorado and Maryland.
- **Teacher qualifications.** For New York, we used the reported percentage of teachers with appropriate teaching certifications or diplomas.

4. School Characteristics

Finally, for each state, we collected and cleaned a battery of variables describing the characteristics of schools, students, and school staff. For all states, this included basic data on student demographics, which are generally made publicly available online, either by the states or by NCES (undated): student enrollment, proportion of students by race and ethnicity, proportion of students eligible for free or reduced-price lunch, proportion of female students, proportion of students with limited English proficiency, proportion of students with disabilities, proportion of students in a gifted program, and proportion of students in an educational development program. We also collected and cleaned data on school type (elementary, etc.) and charter status and, where available, data on principal and teacher years of experience.

Empirical Methodology

Our primary research question of interest is the overall impact of the PPI on outcomes of interest, such as student achievement for schools that received a newly placed principal.[1] The PPI reforms include changes in systems and practices that could potentially affect any school in the district, but that are most likely to affect schools led by newly placed principals in the district. In light of this, we used schools in the state that are outside of the district as controls for the counterfactual year-to-year changes in outcomes absent the pipeline treatment. We used control schools instead of control districts in the state both to increase the quality of matches and to average out interventions happening at the district level in other districts. We investigated how the treatment effect varies year to year after treatment, while not explicitly distinguishing the specific elements of the pipeline to which individual principals have been exposed.

Lacking randomization of principals into schools but given the availability of repeated observations of schools over time, we used quasi-experimental methodology to estimate the causal treatment effect of the principal pipeline. Our primary analysis used a difference-in-difference (DID) multivariate matching regression estimator. We used the approach to estimate to different specifications—a primary one that focuses on schools that get a newly placed principal after PPI implementation and another specification that focuses on all schools in PPI districts as of SY 2012–2013. We begin by describing the approach with reference to the primary specification. We then describe the approach used to estimate district-wide effects.

Estimating the Effect of the PPI on Outcomes

First, we identify schools that are treated by the PPI. In the primary specification, this group includes all schools in PPI districts that get a newly placed principal after SY

---

[1]   Although PPI districts also made investment to enhance the training and support for assistant principals as well as principals, our analysis focused exclusively on the placement and outcomes of newly placed principals. We were not able to obtain data about the placement of new assistant principals in comparison schools.

2011–2012.[2] We then compare the change in outcomes for these treated schools with the change in outcomes for a set of similar comparison schools. We assume that in the absence of the PPI, the change in outcomes over time in the PPI treated schools would follow a similar trajectory to the change in outcomes for similar schools in non-PPI districts in the same state.

We compare changes in outcomes for treated and control schools against the pre-PPI baseline year of 2010–2011. As illustrated in the simplified diagram in Figure B.1, the PPI effect is the extent to which the change in outcomes of treated schools in PPI districts is better (or worse) than that of similar schools in other districts. In the diagram, the treated and control schools start off at the same point—but that need not be the case. The approach adjusts for differences in outcome levels at baseline. Figure B.1 provides a simple overview of our DID approach.

The first step of this is to calculate matching weights. This serves two purposes. First, it removes from the sample schools that either do not have any matches (in the PPI districts) or are not a comparison match for any treated school (in the rest of the state). Second, it also provides regression weights, such that comparison schools that serve as matches for multiple PPI schools receive more weight. We use a one-to-many

Figure B.1
Overview of Difference-in-Difference Approach for Estimating Effects of the PPI

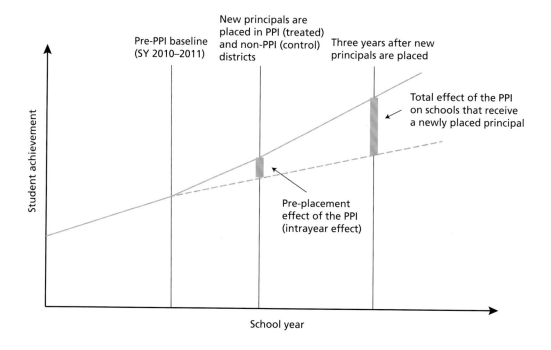

matching algorithm with replacement, meaning that each treatment school is matched with all potential comparison schools within the specified bandwidths. In cases where multiple comparison schools are matched with a given treatment school, each comparison school is assigned a weight that equals the inverse of the number of comparison schools matched to that treatment school. For comparison schools, cumulative weights are generated by adding these weights across all treatment schools. Treatment schools get a weight of 1 if they have at least one control school they match to, and a weight of 0 otherwise. At this stage, we use broad bandwidths on purpose, so as to exclude only schools that are vastly different from the treated schools. The regression model used additional controls for all of the variables matched on, as well as several additional factors. Details are provided in Appendix C.

With the matching weights in hand, we are able to estimate the DID estimator. The model specification for newly placed principals, for outcome z_{it} for school i and year t is given by equation B.1:

$$
\begin{aligned}
z_{it} = \alpha + &\sum_{j=1,2,3+} \beta_j YearsAfterj_{it} \times Post_t \times PPI_i + \\
&\sum_{j=1,2,3+} \gamma_j YearsAfterj_{it} \times Post_t + \lambda_1 Intrayear_{it} + \\
&\lambda_2 Intrayear_{it} \times PPI_i + \sum_{j=1,2,3+} \phi_j YearsAfterj_{it} + \quad \text{(Eq B.1)} \\
&\sum_{j=2007}^{2017} \lambda_j Placed_j + \delta_t + \psi_i + X_{it}\theta + \varepsilon_{it}
\end{aligned}
$$

where

- z_{it}: the outcome
- $YearsAfterj_{it}$: indicator variable for how many years since receiving the first post-2012 newly placed PPI principal (first year, second year, third or later year)
- $Tenurej_{it}$: indicator variable for a principal having been in the school for j years ($j=1,2,3+$) (this term is used in later equations in this appendix)
- $Post_t$: indicator for the school year being after implementation of the PPI (SY 2012–2013 or later)
- $Placed_j$: indicator for the principal having been placed in the new school in year j (for the first year of data, it is equal to the principal having been placed in that year or earlier, given that we cannot observe earlier years and placement dates)
- PPI_i: indicator for being in a PPI district
- $Intrayear_{it}$: indicator for the year being after 2012 but before the first newly placed principal after 2012 arrived
- δ_t: year fixed effects
- ψ_i: school fixed effects

- X_{it}: other school control variables to the extent available by state, including such variables as overall principal experience (in any school), proportion of students eligible the for free or reduced-price lunch program, proportion of students of each race and ethnicity, school type (elementary, etc.), school student enrollment, total district student enrollment, charter status, proportion of students female, proportion of students with limited English proficiency, average experience of the teachers, proportion of students disabled, proportion of students in a gifted program, proportion of students with an educational development program, and rurality of the location of the school.

The treatment effect is captured by the three β_j coefficients, of which we focus and report on the second year and third-plus year treatment effects as well as the intra-year effect. The total PPI effect on newly placed principals is the relative change in outcomes for treated versus control schools 2 or 3+ years after the placement of new principals compared with the pre-PPI baseline year. The *Intrayear* effect captures the relative change that occurs before the new principals are placed. That timeframe may be one, two, three, or four years, depending on the cohort and effect being analyzed. The total PPI effect captures the total difference in performance both before and after the newly placed principals are placed. The pre-placement differences could be due to district-wide effects of the PPI or to changes in how PPI districts manage principal transitions before and during the transition. Prior research (Miller, 2013) found that schools experience declines in achievement prior to a principal transition that continue for the first two years of a new principal's tenure.

The school fixed effects control for the different levels of the outcome across schools before treatment. The year fixed effects control for common shifts in the outcome in each year. Thus, the change in outcomes in the control schools before the newly placed principal serves as a counterfactual for the change in outcomes for the treated schools. For missing covariates, we interpolate within school where possible, and set the covariate equal to the sample average otherwise, and include in the regression an indicator for that variable being imputed for that school in that year. We restrict the set of schools using the multivariate matching algorithm and include the resulting weights in this regression, as described in Appendix C. We cluster standard errors at the district level to be most conservative.

To aggregate from the district estimates to an overall effect estimate, we take the simple average of the six district estimates. This framing focuses on the implications of districts implementing a set of practices with some additional resources and support, with the idea that each district is an independent test of the PPI. The answer sheds light on how much other districts might benefit if they took the same steps as the PPI districts and could access the same supports. The approach also avoids the one larger district driving the overall outcomes. We performed sensitivity checks where we ran a pooled analysis. To do so, we put all states' observations into one regression. For any control variables not present in every state, we created an indicator variable for the missing status of the variable and set missing values equal to 0. We also included state fixed effects. The pooled analysis yielded slightly larger treatment effects than the averaged analysis we used in this report, with similar significance.

For the student achievement outcomes, we use the treatment effects as the standardized z-scores by year, subject, grade, and state. We then convert the treatment effects into marginal percentile points by taking the standard normal cumulative density function of the coefficient and multiplying this by 100.

When performing inference between two subgroups (e.g., new district hires versus reassigned principals), we assume independence between the two estimates in question and thus estimate the standard error of the difference as the square root of the sum of the squares of the standard errors of the two estimates. This is necessary because both estimates are averages across districts, and calculating the covariance between the two estimates would require a pooling of the data across districts and estimation on this super-sample, a method we are not confident in. We have no strong priors in any given case regarding which direction the covariance would be, and thus are unable to make statements regarding whether our independence assumption is likely to lead to larger or smaller p-values for the t-tests of the differences.

Independent of the definition of treatment, controlling for principal tenure is important. Research indicates that schools with first-time principals fare worse than those with more-experienced principals in terms of student achievement gains (Clark, Martorell, and Rockoff, 2009). Analyzing first-time principals avoids the criticism of having cumulative leadership effects distort student gains (Grissom, Kalogrides, and Loeb, 2015). As such, where available, we controlled for overall principal experience as an additional covariate in our model.

An alternative specification considers whether there are district-wide effects of the PPI on all schools in PPI districts. To do so, we used the same specification shown in equation B.1, with a few changes. Equation B.2 presents this specification. *Post2012* is a variable denoting whether it is one year after the 2011–2012 school year, two years after, or three or more years after. All other variables are defined above. All treated schools are matched against all schools in the state based on 2010–2011 characteristics, and all schools are included.

$$
\begin{aligned}
z_{it} = \alpha + \sum_{j=1,2,3+} & \beta_j Post2012j_{it} \times PPI_i + \\
\sum_{j=1,2,3+} & \gamma_j Post2012j_{jt} + \\
\sum_{j=2007}^{2017} & \lambda_j Placed_j + \delta_t + \psi_i + X_{it}\theta + \varepsilon_{it}
\end{aligned}
\qquad \text{(Eq B.2)}
$$

We investigated several additional outcomes other than student achievement. For all but principal retention, we used the same specification as shown in equation B.1. For principal retention, we cannot use the same methodology, given that the outcome is not observed in all years. For example, for some treated schools, we may observe principal retention only into the second year after placement after 2012, by not having a newly placed principal in the data years before 2011. Therefore, we cannot use a school fixed effects DID estimator. Instead, we matched schools on demographics but not on average outcomes. We calculated the average principal retention (*MeanZ*) in the pre-2012 period, and where it was missing, we used the district average for the only district the school came from. We then include one observation per school—whether the first newly placed principal after 2012 was still in place in the second year or third year (for these separate outcomes). Equation B.3 describes this.

$$z_i = \alpha + \beta PPI_i + \gamma MeanZ_i + X_{it}\theta + \varepsilon_{it}. \qquad \text{(Eq B.3)}$$

Exploratory Analysis of Relationship Between PPI Effects and PPI Components

While there is great interest in understanding whether particular components of principal pipelines might be driving effects, the nature of the PPI and its implementation posed a number of challenges for the identification of such causal relationships. Nevertheless, given the rich data we had available, we explored correlations between PPI effects and components as a way to identify interesting patterns that might be worthy of further research. These analyses are highly exploratory in nature. Because they are not designed for causal inference, we do not correct for multiple comparisons. Broadly speaking, our analyses of the correlations between treatment effects and PPI components fall into two main categories: analysis of district-wide effects in the year(s) following implementation of PPI components, and analysis of effects correlated with individual principals' exposure with specific experiences or systems related to the individual PPI components. In Table B.1, we detail for each component what exploratory analyses we consider, and what questions those analyses inform. We also clarify what we can and cannot infer from the corresponding results.

In all cases of our analysis of mechanisms, we look for evidence of PPI components that appear correlated with larger or smaller treatment effect estimates, either at the individual school level or aggregated to the district-by-year level, depending on the analysis. If results are neither positive nor negative, that simply implies that a component contributed similarly to other components to the overall effects of the PPI. All of our analyses include controls for the average effects estimated for each district, which means we are focusing on factors that explain the variation in relative effect sizes within each of the districts. A positive or negative finding indicates that a component

Table B.1. Summary of Exploratory Analyses Regarding PPI Components

PPI Component	Exploratory Analysis Type and Questions	Interpretation	Key Caveats
Leader standards	District-by-year level: Does the timing of substantial district-wide reforms to leader standards correspond to the size of PPI effects?	Larger district-wide effects following implementation of these reforms may indicate the contribution of the reforms.	Reforms may take time to affect student learning, biasing our findings downward as we measure all pre-versus-post differences. We might also pick up on other PPI reforms that kick in not long after these reforms.
Preferred preservice and residencies	School level: Do schools led by new principals hired from districts' "preferred" preservice programs and/or from programs with residencies exhibit larger PPI effects?[a]	Preservice programs and residencies that have key characteristics recommended by the PPI may yield stronger principal candidates.	Nonpreferred programs may be stronger on other unobserved dimensions; hiring screens may level the playing field even if preservice programs vary in quality. Results do not reflect districts where all principals came from a preferred or residency program.
Selective hiring processes	School level: Do new principals who were part of a district "talent pool" process exhibit larger PPI effects? Do the talent pool ratings themselves predict more effective principals?	Participation in a talent pool process at hiring, as well as any talent pool ratings, may correspond to principals who were more selectively screened and thus more effective.	We do not observe the effectiveness of those principals screened out by talent pools and never hired, which may be the primary way in which selection screens influence the quality of new hires.
Evaluation reforms	District-by-year level: Does the timing of substantial district-wide reforms to evaluation systems correspond to the size of PPI effects?	Larger district-wide effects following implementation of these reforms may indicate the contribution of the reforms.	Reforms may take time to affect student learning, biasing our findings downward as we measure all pre-versus-post differences. We might also pick up on other PPI reforms that kick in not long after these reforms.
Induction supports	School level: Do schools led by new principals who received either induction PD or induction mentoring exhibit larger PPI effects?	Receipt of induction supports might boost new principal effectiveness, all other things being equal.	Receipt of induction PD or mentoring may be most common among principals who need help. Negative selection may bias estimates.

NOTE: Leader standards and evaluation reform analyses include just four PPI districts where substantial changes in these practices occurred during the course of the study. The analysis of associations with individuals' talent pool scores (but not overall talent pool participation) included only five districts based on data availability. All other analyses included all six districts.

[a] Following Turnbull, Anderson, et al. (2016), we define a residency as a clinical experience for an aspiring leader that takes place in a new setting other than their current position. Turnbull, Anderson, et al. (2016) found that the duration of the residency for preferred programs in PPI partner districts varied from a month to an entire school year (p. 19).

may have had a larger or smaller effect relative to other potential contributors to the overall effects of the PPI within each district.

For the analysis that relates the treatment effects at the school level to the PPI components the principals had been exposed to, the regression is specified as the school-level treatment effects regressed on an indicator for whether they had been exposed to each component, as well as district fixed effects. Specifically, the treatment effect of school i in PPI district d, $\widehat{\beta_{id}}$, is specified by

$$
\begin{aligned}
\widehat{\beta_{id}} = \alpha &+ \gamma_1 Comp_1 + \gamma_{2a} Comp_{2a} + \gamma_{2b} Comp_{2b} + \\
&\gamma_3 Comp_3 + \gamma_{4a} Comp_{4a} + \gamma_{4b} Comp_{4b} + \gamma_{4c} Comp_{4c} + \psi_d + \varepsilon_{id}
\end{aligned}
\qquad \text{(Eq B.4)}
$$

where the component indicators are defined by

- $Comp_1$: Leadership standards
- $Comp_{2a}$: Preferred preservice
- $Comp_{2b}$: Residency
- $Comp_3$: Participation in a talent pool
- $Comp_{3a}$: Talent pool score
- $Comp_{4a}$: Evaluation
- $Comp_{4b}$: Induction personal development
- $Comp_{4c}$: Induction mentoring.

We also perform the regressions with one component at a time, as well as state fixed effects, in order to identify the unadjusted associations of each component in isolation.[3] We evaluate for all placed principals, and separately for new to district principals.[4] The components are either classified at the individual principal level (for components 2, 3, and 4b and 4c) or the district/year level (for components 1 and 4a). The components are defined in detail in Appendix A.

For the analysis that relates the treatment effects at the school level to the characteristics of the schools, we do subgroup regression by evaluating the main specification (equation B.1) for a certain subgroup of the treatment group (e.g., all schools with over 50 percent of students who are non-white). We also employ the model specified in equation B.4 by regressing the school-level treatment effects on the school characteristics in the year prior to placement of the principal, as well as district fixed effects. The characteristics we investigate are proportion of the school with race that is non-white,

---

[3]   For component 3a, talent pool scores, we only consider a model with univariate outcomes since this component measure is unique in being a continuous (rather than binary) measure score linked to each school and relates to principal characteristics rather than to exposure to a particular PPI component.

[4]   We had insufficient sample size of reassigned principals to conduct a robust investigation of component effects in that group, but we were able to examine the new to district principals in isolation.

the proportion of the school's students eligible for the free or reduced-price lunch program, the school's student enrollment number, whether the school is a charter school or not, and the baseline average mathematics and reading scores.

Sensitivity Checks

Sensitivity checks allowed us to explore how sensitive our results are to key assumptions in the main analytical approach.

Our DID model relies on an assumption that, absent the PPI, the outcomes of schools in PPI districts would follow a similar trajectory as the outcomes of similar schools in non-PPI districts. A standard way to validate this assumption is by checking whether the trends are similar in the pre-treatment period as in the post-treatment period. Because the PPI included districts that had already implemented some of the pipeline activities prior to the launch of the initiative, this approach to validating the assumptions of the DID model has limitations. In this case, differences in pre-treatment trends might reflect the effects of this pre-initiative implementation. We examined trends in achievement between treatment and control schools, and there were some states where pre-treatment trends in PPI districts may have differed from those observed in control schools. Normally, if trends are not similar in the pre-treatment and post-treatment period, the comparative interrupted time series (CITS) can be considered. This approach corrects for pre-treatment trends—effectively assuming that they are unrelated to treatment and therefore something to control for in the analysis. We did a sensitivity check, running the analysis using a CITS approach. The results were qualitatively similar to those reported here.

We ran CITS allowing for trends that differ for treatment and control. The pattern of results was similar: positive and statistically significant. In fact, similar to the test of pooled versus the aggregated treatment effects, the CITS overall results were uniformly larger than our DID approach, such that our preferred and presented methodology presents the more conservative estimate between the two. This, in and of itself, as well as the simpler nature of DID, constitute part of our preference for DID over CITS. Additionally, it is not clear that CITS is well suited to this evaluation, because the timing of implementation is not clear-cut. Districts were selected in part because of activities that they already had underway—so it would not be surprising if these districts were already on a path to better outcomes in say 2010 or 2011. Insofar as this is true, it would lead to downward-biased results from the DID as we assign to pre-treatment years newly placed principals with partial treatment. We are unable to with confidence designate the start of exposure to any of the pipeline elements for each district, and thus prefer instead to work with the start of the PPI relationship, and not make explicit modeling assumptions of this timing and trajectories so as to correct for it in the analysis, as would be done with CITS. Thus, and again given that the results are similar, we prefer the original approach.

As discussed earlier, we also tested a model in which we pooled all of the states and ran one regression across the states including state fixed effects, instead of regressing each state separately and then averaging. This required us to adjust for different covariates present across states, which we did by creating missing indicators and setting any missing equal to 0. The pooled regression yielded slightly larger treatment effects, and slightly larger standard errors, with the same interpretation of positive and statistically significant effects of the PPI on student achievement.

We tested various alternative matching bandwidths. We found that as long as the bands were not overly restrictive and tight, the results were not significantly changed. This is likely due to the doubly robust nature of our analysis, where the second stage regression still adjusted for all of the covariates in the same way. The results with very tight bandwidths became more extreme, in some cases for larger treatment effects and in other cases smaller, with larger standard errors due to the highly restricted sample.

Because of the way the PPI was implemented, there is no clear separation between pre-treatment from post-treatment, either for a given school or for the district as a whole. We replicated the main analysis under alternative assumptions about when principals in PPI districts would experience effects of the PPI efforts. To test the possibility that the effects kicked in before or after SY 2012–2013, we ran the analyses assuming the first treatment year was, for example, SY 2009–2010. We tested this for every year, before and after the 2012–2013 year used in the main analysis. We did this both for the analysis that considers only newly placed principals to be treated and for the analysis that considers all principals to be treated. In both cases, there was some evidence of the estimated treatment effects increasing starting around SY 2012–2013, based on smaller counter-factual treatment effect estimates for years prior to SY 2012–2013 and a visible jump in the treatment effects around SY 2012–2013.

We also performed an analysis that includes charter schools for all districts, as well as the non-charter schools, even for PPI districts that do not have jurisdiction over the charter schools. This sensitivity check aims to gauge whether our findings are meaningfully influenced by independently managed schools that may have been less directly affected by the PPI reforms. The results were almost exactly the same, which is due to the fact that even when these districts have jurisdiction over charter schools, it comprises a small portion of their pool of schools.

Finally, we evaluated how sensitive the results are to the inclusion of newly opened schools by dropping these schools from the analysis. This sensitivity check assesses the extent to which our findings are dependent on schools for which we lack a lengthy historical record of performance that we can control for our models. The results were again very similar.

We also estimated an alternative version of the main approach that uses the immediate pre-placement baseline year—the year just before the new principals are placed—as the reference point against which treated and control principals are evaluated. The model specification outcome z_{it} for school i and year t is given by equation

B.5. The treatment estimates from this specification tended to be smaller, which is not surprising given that it includes in the "pre" period for PPI districts some years that are after the implementation of PPI district-wide but before the school received the newly placed principal. As shown, there were positive district-wide effects, so that inclusion of these years in the "pre" period for PPI schools would decrease the difference between pre and post, decreasing also the estimated treatment effects.

$$z_{it} = \alpha + \sum_{j=1,2,3+} \beta_j YearsAfterj_{it} \times Post_t \times PPI_i +$$
$$\sum_{j=1,2,3+} \gamma_j Tenurej_{jt} + \sum_{j=2007}^{2017} \lambda_j Placed_j + \delta_t + \psi_i + X_{it}\theta + \varepsilon_{it}$$

(Eq B.5)

Matching Algorithm

This appendix supplements the information provided in Chapter Two on the matching algorithm. We use a multivariate matching DID estimator to estimate year-by-year treatment effects. Similar schools throughout the state that also received newly placed principals serve as the control group for this analysis. In examining effects, we look at the changes in outcomes (e.g., student achievement) upon receiving a newly placed principal rather than the outcome levels. The DID estimator contrasts changes in outcomes for treated schools before and after PPI treatment to the concurrent change in outcomes for control schools. Multivariate matching restricts the comparison sample to schools in other parts of the state that also received a new principal in the same year as the treated school as well as the treatment group to schools with at least one match in the comparison group. The matching strategy requires that comparison schools are the same as treated schools on three critical dimensions and similar to the treated schools on other dimensions for which exact matching was not feasible:

- same year of placement: exact match
- whether the school is a newly opened school: exact match
- same school type (e.g., elementary): exact match
- baseline fraction of students eligible for free or reduced-price lunch: within 33.3 percentage points
- baseline fraction minority student population: within 50 percentage points
- baseline outcome
  - standardized test scores within 0.3 standard deviations
  - for principal retention outcome, we do not match on baseline principal retention
  - all other outcomes matched within one standard deviation of the outcome across all schools.

These matching criteria were chosen so that treated and comparison schools would be expected to experience similar outcome trajectories based on the factors that have been empirically related to outcomes. Research has shown that achievement outcomes decline with the placement of a new principal so we only chose comparison schools that also received a newly placed principal in the same year as the treated school. The newly opened school was selected because in these cases, we cannot control in the same way for prior data (and importantly, for baseline outcomes), and newly opened schools might face different challenges. Baseline outcomes are important given trajectories of the outcome may differ depending on the starting point.

We use multivariate matching, which is to say that for any given treatment school, only comparison schools that fall within the bandwidth on every criterion is retained. We use moderately sized bandwidths for the matching because the purpose of the matching strategy is to remove schools from the sample that do not resemble at all any of the schools in the PPI district that received new principals, as well as any treated school for which there is not even an approximately adequate comparison school across these important dimensions. We then control for all of these variables, as well as several others, in the regression analysis. Most importantly, we control for school and time fixed effects, which identifies the effects based on changes in the outcomes. We do not use smaller bandwidths because, given the multivariate matching algorithm, it is easy to end up with very small or empty comparison groups for a given school if the bandwidths are too small. However, the second step, namely the DID regression, adjusts much more precisely for all of these measures as well as several others. The matching process is used as a first step primarily to remove obviously bad matches from the analytic sample.

The matching algorithm then generates weights for the subsequent regressions. Weights of zero are given to treatment schools with no matches in the control group, as well as control schools with no matches in the treatment group. Weights of one are given to treatment schools with at least one comparison school match. For comparison schools with at least one match in the treatment group, the weights for school i is given by

$$weight_i = \sum_{j \in treatment} \frac{1(i \in match\ set\ for\ j)}{\sum_{k \in control} 1(k \in match\ set\ for\ j)}.$$

The denominator is for each treatment school the number of comparison schools it matches to. For each comparison school, this is then summed up across each treatment school it matches to. This then is a version of coarsened exact matching using moving calipers for the bandwidths on the continuous measures that are discretized, a method that has been shown to outperform univariate matching methods such as propensity score matching (see Iacus, King, and Porro, 2012). In combination with the subsequent regression analysis, this forms a type of doubly robust estimator, which by improving the balance of the regression through matching improves several properties of the estimator over simply doing the regression (see Bang and Robins, 2005).

Matching was conducted one-to-many with replacement, meaning that each treatment school is matched with all potential comparison schools within the specified bandwidth. In cases where multiple comparison schools are matched with a treatment school, each comparison school is assigned a weight that equals the inverse of the number of comparison schools matched to that treatment school. For comparison schools, cumulative weights are generated by adding these weights across all treatment schools; treatment schools get a weight of 1 if they have at least one control school they match to, and a weight of 0 otherwise.

We did test the sensitivity of our results to different choices of bin sizes. Broader bin sizes yielded very similar results, likely due to the doubly robust nature of our analysis, which follows matching with the multivariate regression, controlling for the variables. However, significantly narrower bins did in some cases lead to somewhat different results, given the high restrictiveness put on some schools, leading to excessive dropping of treated schools. For example, in some states, narrower bin sizes led to the exclusion of certain types of schools from the analysis. Notably, in some states, it was not possible to find matches for PPI district schools that served a high percentage of minority or free or reduced-price lunch students and were also relatively high performing at baseline. Given that our approach includes controls for school characteristics, we preferred to include such schools with weaker matches rather than drop them from the analysis entirely. That said, our overall findings were not highly sensitive to this choice.

Figure C.1 reports the matching fractions. There are good matches across all districts, leading to our retention of 80 to 100 percent of all treated schools. We also retain over half of the comparison schools that have a newly placed principal.

Figure C.2 presents the baseline achievement scores. We estimated baseline equivalence according to the What Works Clearinghouse approach. For schools that receive a newly placed principal in the study period, we calculate the weighted difference in average scores between treated schools and control schools in SY 2010–2011 divided by the pooled standard deviation of the scores to be 0.045 for mathematics and 0.031 for reading, well within the 0.25 rule of thumb for claims of baseline equivalence between the treatment and chosen comparison groups. The matched sample tends to be a closer match to the treated sample than overall in the state. The same is true for free and reduced-price lunch eligibility proportions and minority proportions (not reported here, but available upon request). Thus, the first step of matching to observationally similar schools does accomplish its goal of improving similarity of comparison schools while still retaining approximately 60–90 percent of the comparison schools in the state for the more carefully adjusted second step of regression analysis.

Figure C.1
Proportion of Schools That Have at Least One Match

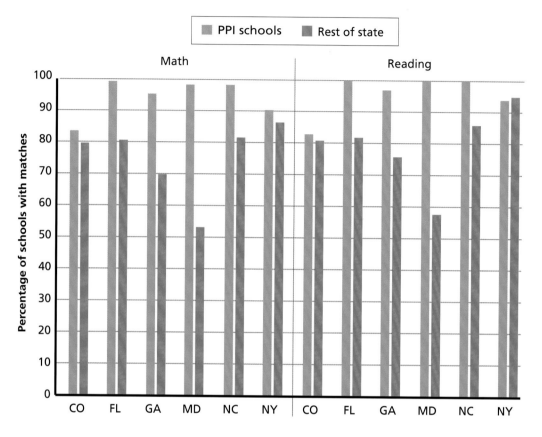

Figure C.2
Matched Baseline Achievement Scores

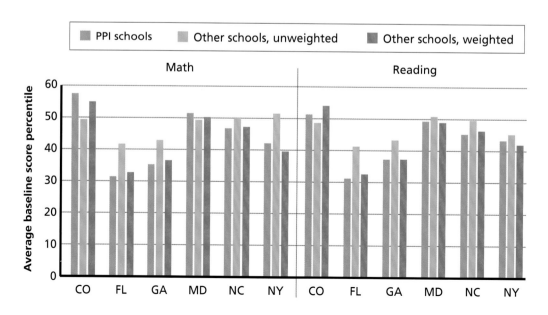

Supplementary Tables and Figures

In this appendix, we provide several additional tables and figures that, while helpful in understanding the PPI intervention, were omitted from the main text in favor of concision. These include additional results for supplementary descriptive statistics, main analysis, sensitivity analysis, and exploratory analysis. Our supplementary exploratory analysis comprises heterogeneity of treatment effects, analysis of additional outcomes, and component mechanism analysis.

Descriptive Statistics

Figure D.1 presents the proportion of principals in each year who are newly placed, both within the PPI district and across the rest of the state for that district. There is variation over time and between PPI and non-PPI schools, but the rates tend to fall in the 0.1 to 0.2 (10 percent to 20 percent) range overall. The third (middle left) district in the figure has the most dramatic increase in retention around the time of the start of the PPI.

Figure D.1
Proportion of Schools with a Newly Placed Principal in Each Year, by District

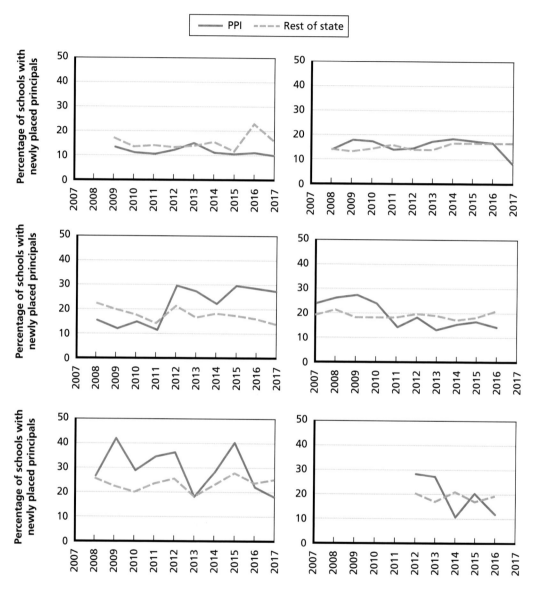

NOTES: The charts for each state are presented in order (from left to right and top to bottom) from lowest to highest initial PPI percentage.

Figure D.2 presents the raw average scores for all schools in PPI districts, and not just schools with newly placed principals. Given achievement is standardized to the state, we omit the comparison schools, recognizing the 50th percentile as the relevant baseline of average state achievement. There is wide variation across sites, with some districts averaging close to the 30th percentile and one district averaging around the 60th percentile. We see some improvement over time in these raw scores in some districts, most dramatically for the district indicated by the green line (lowermost in 2007) in both subjects and the districts indicated by the brown and orange lines (the second- and third-lowermost in 2007) for reading.

Figure D.2
Average Achievement, by PPI District

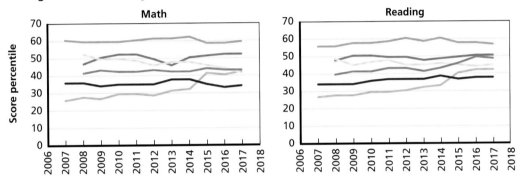

Figure D.3 shows the raw two-year retention trends for newly placed principals in PPI districts compared with the rest of the state.

Figure D.3
Two-Year Retention for Newly Placed Principals in PPI Districts and the Rest of the State

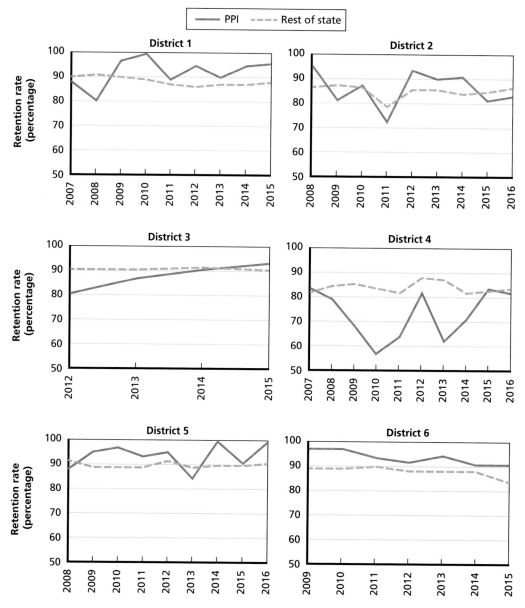

Main Analysis

We next turn to supplementary results for our main analysis. In the bar charts that follow, the bars indicate the point estimates for the effects, and the vertical lines indicate 95 percent confidence intervals—meaning that there is a 95 percent probability the actual effect falls in the range of the vertical lines.

Figure D.4 shows the main effects results presented in Figure 4.1, as well as the *intrayear* effect, which captures the effect of the PPI on treated schools in the years prior to the placement of a new principal. Our analysis is based on a total sample of 1,128 treated and 6,364 control schools for which we have either mathematics achievement scores, reading achievement scores or both.

Figure D.4
Main Effects of the PPI on Student Achievement

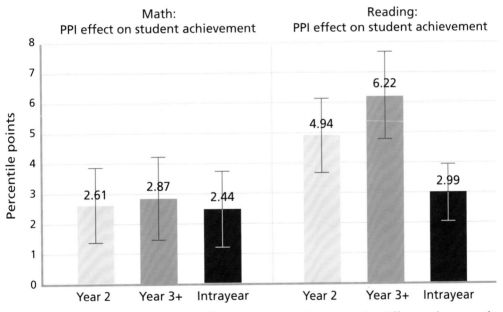

NOTES: The numerals indicate the *PPI effect* on student achievement: the difference between the percentile point change in achievement for schools in PPI districts and similar schools in other districts. The change in achievement is measured here between the baseline year (SY 2010–2011) and either two or three+ years after the placement of a new principal, as in Figure 4.1. This figure also shows the intrayear effect: the effect of the PPI on treated schools in the years prior to the placement of a new principal. As the error lines indicate, these effects are statistically significant at the 5-percent level.

Figure D.5 shows the cohort estimates of the achievement treatment effects for reassigned principals as a complement to Figure 4.9 for new district hires.

Figure D.5
Achievement Treatment Effect, by Cohort, for Reassigned Principals

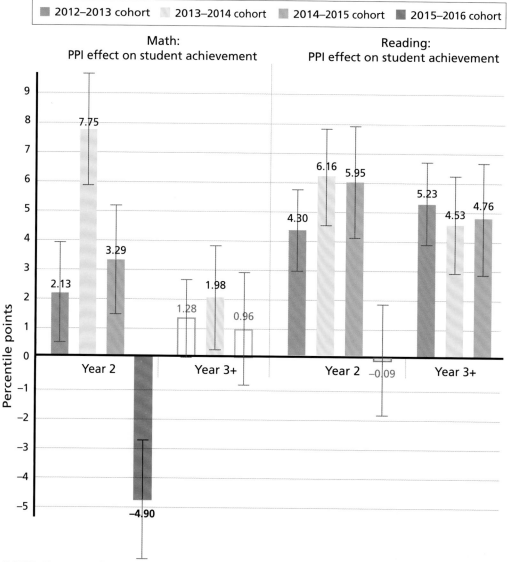

NOTES: The numerals indicate the *PPI effect* on student achievement: the difference between the percentile point change in achievement for schools in PPI districts and similar schools in other districts. The change in achievement is measured here between the baseline year (SY 2010–2011) and either two or three+ years after placement of a reassigned principal, and the effects are broken down by cohort, defined in terms of the SY in which the new principal was hired. These effects are statistically significant at the 5-percent level, except where indicated by the error lines, hollow (white) bars, and gray numerals.

Figure D.6 shows effects of the PPI on two-year and three-year principal retention, by cohort.

Figure D.6
Effects of the PPI on Two-Year and Three-Year Principal Retention, by Cohort

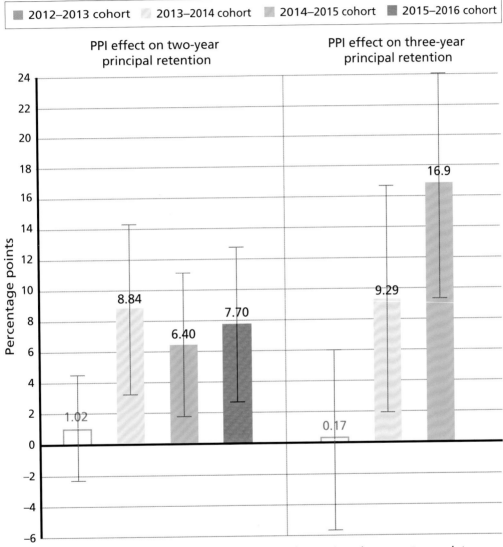

NOTES: The numerals indicate the *PPI effect* on principal retention: the percentage point difference between principal retention in PPI districts and similar schools in non-PPI districts. Retention is measured two and three years after the placement of a new principal, and the effects are broken down by cohort, defined in terms of the SY in which the new principal was hired. The effects here are statistically significant at the 5-percent level, except where indicated by the error lines, hollow (white) bars, and gray text.

Figure D.7 shows the principal retention treatment effects by whether the newly placed principal is a new hire or a reassigned principal. Consistent with the hypothesis, new district hires have larger treatment effects.

Figure D.7
Effects of the PPI on Principal Retention for New District Hires Versus Reassigned Principals

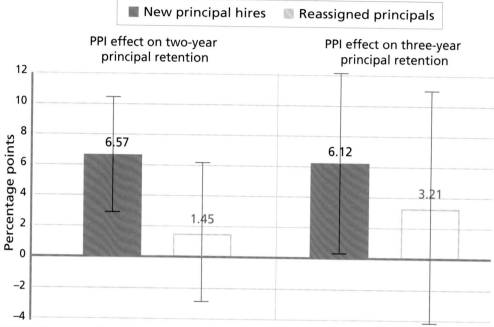

NOTES: The numerals indicate the *PPI effect* on principal retention: the percentage point difference between principal retention in PPI districts and similar schools in non-PPI districts. Retention is measured two and three years after the placement of a new principal, and the effects are broken down by whether the newly placed principals in the PPI districts were new hires or reassigned from other principalships in the district. A caveat is that, for the comparison group, we could not identify the subgroups of schools that had new principal hires or reassigned principals, so here we compare the outcomes for the PPI subgroups against outcomes for all newly placed principals in the comparison schools. These effects are statistically significant at the 5-percent level for new district hires.

Exploratory Analysis

We next present the results that investigate how the effects differ by school characteristics, with specific attention to whether the schools are disadvantaged or not across various measures. We first examine the results according to the proportion of the schools that are eligible for the free and reduced-price lunch program. Disadvantage for free and reduced-price lunch eligibility has been at times defined for schools with over 50 percent eligible as well as for schools with over 75 percent eligible (U.S. Department of Education, 2018b). Figure D.8 presents these results. For both mathematics and reading, there is a clear downward trajectory where schools with higher proportions of free and reduced-price lunch eligible students have smaller treatment effects. In fact, for mathematics, schools with 50 percent or more free and reduced-price lunch eligible students as well as 75 percent or more have small and statistically insignificant effects.

Figure D.8
Treatment Effects, by Proportion of Students Eligible for Free or Reduced-Price Lunch

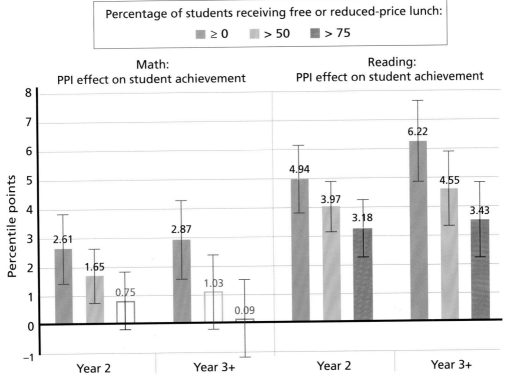

NOTES: The numerals indicate the *PPI effect* on student achievement: the difference between the percentile point change in achievement for schools in PPI districts and similar schools in other districts. The change in achievement is measured here between the baseline year (SY 2010–2011) and either two or three+ years after placement of a reassigned principal, and the effects are broken down by the percentage of students who are eligible for a free or reduced-price lunch. These effects are statistically significant at the 5-percent level, except where indicated by the error lines, hollow (white) bars, and gray numerals.

We next look at the results for the fraction of the students who are nonwhite. We use the same comparative thresholds of 50 percent or more nonwhite (Education Week Research Center, 2018) and 75 percent or more nonwhite (U.S. Department of Education, 2007). Similar to free and reduced-price lunch, we find that schools with high proportions of nonwhite students have smaller treatment effects than schools with lower proportions, as shown in Figure D.9. This is again especially true for mathematics.

We examine how the estimated treatment effects differ by the baseline achievement of the school. To do so, we look at where the baseline scores fall in the state distribution of scores. This is simply done given we have converted scores to percentiles; we are able to look at schools whose scores are in the first quartile (1st to 24th percentile), second quartile (25th to 49th percentile), third quartile (50th to 74th percentile), and fourth quartile (75th to 99th percentile). Figure D.10 shows how many schools fall in each quartile. Approximately half of all schools fall in the second quartile. Another

Figure D.9
Treatment Effects, by Proportion of Students Who Are Nonwhite

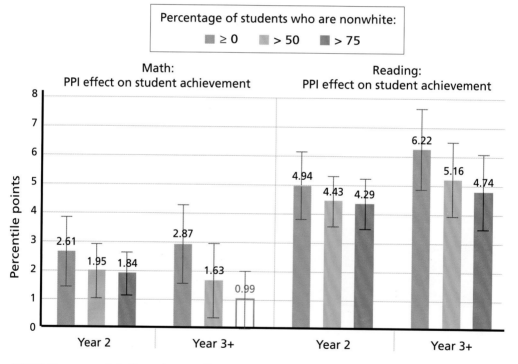

NOTES: The numerals indicate the *PPI effect* on student achievement: the difference between the percentile point change in achievement for schools in PPI districts and similar schools in other districts. The change in achievement is measured here between the baseline year (SY 2010–2011) and either two or three+ years after placement of a reassigned principal, and the effects are broken down by the percentage of students in schools who are nonwhite. These effects are statistically significant at the 5-percent level, except where indicated by the error lines, hollow (white) bars, and gray numerals.

Figure D.10
Proportion of Schools in Each Baseline Achievement Quartile

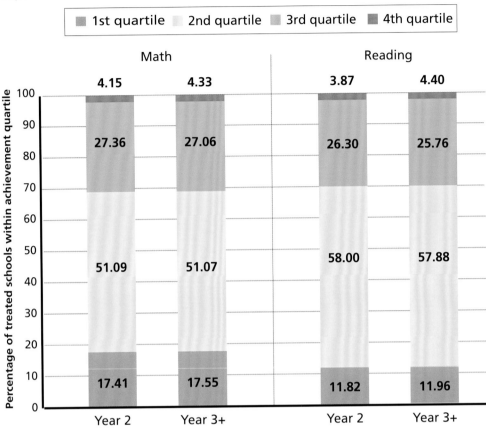

quarter fall in the third quartile, about 20 percent in the first quartile, and about 5 percent are in the fourth quartile.

Figure D.11 presents the treatment effects by baseline quartile of the statewide achievement distribution. The smallest treatment effects are for the second quartile, while the largest effects tend to be for the lowest and highest quartiles. This may reflect for example that treatment effects are larger for the less disadvantaged schools (higher quartiles), but also that the districts target and try to send better principals to the lowest-achieving schools.

We also investigate these results through by-school regressions. To do this, we estimate treatment effects for each treated school and then regress their treatment effect on the characteristics of the schools. These analyses shed light on the relationship between school characteristics and the size of PPI effects among treated schools in PPI districts and allow us to consider whether some types of schools had larger effects than others. Table D.1 presents these regression findings. These suggest that, overall, assuming a linear relationship between these characteristics and effects, the size of the

Figure D.11
Treatment Effects, by Baseline Achievement Quartile

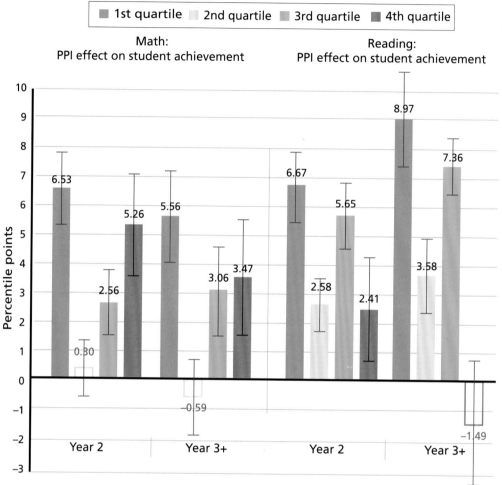

NOTES: The numerals indicate the *PPI effect* on student achievement: the difference between the percentile point change in achievement for schools in PPI districts and similar schools in other districts. The change in achievement is measured here between the baseline year (SY 2010–2011) and either two or three+ years after placement of a reassigned principal, and the effects are broken down by the baseline score quartile in the state. These effects are statistically significant at the 5-percent level, except where indicated by the error lines, hollow (white) bars, and gray numerals.

PPI effects were smaller as the proportion of nonwhite students, students eligible for free and reduced-price lunch, and school enrollment increased. The results here are consistent with the subgroup regression results presented in Figures D.8–D.11. The results also suggest that schools with higher baseline reading scores experienced smaller PPI effects.

We next present findings related to all of the outcomes investigated. Table D.2 defines the outcomes investigated, as well as the number of districts for which we can

Table D.1
Regressions of School Treatment Effects on School Characteristics

	All	Mathematics	Reading	Transfer Principals	Novice Principals	Univariate Regressions
% Nonwhite	−31.27***	−37.37***	−25.67***	−47.54**	−17.81	−28.51***
	(7.055)	(10.45)	(9.301)	(22.38)	(10.96)	(4.169)
% FRL	−31.90***	−39.12***	−25.28***	−17.05	−20.04*	−21.27***
	(7.259)	(11.03)	(9.049)	(25.38)	(10.49)	(3.931)
Enrollment	−0.00388**	−0.00322	−0.00456**	−0.00285	−0.00112	−0.00302*
	(0.00171)	(0.00252)	(0.00231)	(0.00496)	(0.00300)	(0.00165)
Charter school	−16.57	−16.05	−16.20	17.72	3.201	−22.35**
	(10.58)	(15.15)	(14.85)	(10.95)	(7.189)	(10.34)
Math baseline percentile	−0.0754	−0.192	−0.00690	−0.845*	0.0109	−0.0730
	(0.131)	(0.200)	(0.166)	(0.455)	(0.188)	(0.0534)
Reading baseline percentiles	−0.575***	−0.593***	−0.522**	0.211	−0.456**	−0.103*
	(0.158)	(0.228)	(0.211)	(0.503)	(0.231)	(0.0608)
Observations	1,919	953	966	220	781	—
R-squared	0.116	0.137	0.148	0.156	0.131	—

NOTES: Standard errors are in parentheses. * $p < 0.1$, ** $p < 0.05$, *** $p < 0.01$.

estimate the model on that outcome. Table D.3 presents all of the treatment effects using the main model, across several outcomes. The overall findings are summarized in Tables 4.1 and 4.2 in Chapter Four.

Next we turn to how our treatment effect estimates are related to which components of the pipeline the principal had been exposed to. As explained in Appendix B, we do this by estimating school-level treatment effects, and then regressing these effects on the components.

Table D.4 presents these results for the achievement effect estimates, which do not control for multiple hypotheses. In the analysis that includes all newly placed principals and controls for all components simultaneously, we find few correlations between components and treatment effects. We observe a weak negative correlation between exposure to the talent pool and effects, but because we have not controlled for multiple comparisons, that could be due to chance. A regression analysis limited to reassigned principals shows a strong positive correlation between implementation of evaluation component and positive effects. This could suggest that, after implementing new evaluation approaches, PPI districts were more likely to reassign high-performing principals. A regression analysis limited to new district hires shows a negative effect

Table D.2
Definition of All Investigated Outcomes

Outcome	Number of Districts	Definition
Math percentile scores	6	Achievement scores for students on math tests
Reading percentile scores	6	Achievement scores for students on reading tests
Science percentile scores	3	Achievement scores for students on science tests
Social studies percentile scores	1	Achievement scores for students on social studies tests
Attendance rate	5	Average rate of attendance of students
Climate rating (1–5)	1	Overall climate rating surveys on 1 to 5 scale, aggregating scores for climate survey, discipline records, safe and substance free environment, and attendance (students and teachers)
Principal's average climate rating (1–4)	1	Principals' average survey responses on the following: (1) effectiveness of the school solving problems, (2) an atmosphere of trust and mutual respect in the school, (3) teachers feeling comfortable raising issues and concerns that are important to them, (4) the school leadership consistently supporting teachers, (5) teachers being held to high professional standards for delivering instruction, (6) the school improvement team providing effective leadership at this school, and (7) overall, the school being a good place to work and learn
Principal's rating of overall school climate (1–4)	1	Principals' responses on: Overall, my school is a good place to work and learn
Teacher's average climate rating (1–4)	1	Teachers' average survey responses on the following: (1) effectiveness of the school solving problems, (2) an atmosphere of trust and mutual respect in the school, (3) teachers feeling comfortable raising issues and concerns that are important to them, (4) the school leadership consistently supporting teachers, (5) teachers being held to high professional standards for delivering instruction, (6) the school improvement team providing effective leadership at this school, and (7) overall, the school being a good place to work and learn
Teacher's rating of overall school climate (1–4)	1	Teachers' responses on: Overall, my school is a good place to work and learn
Graduation rate	3	Graduation rate for high schools
Principal retention (2 years)	6	Indicator for the principal being present in their second year after placement
Principal retention (3 years)	6	Indicator for the principal being present in their third year after placement
Teacher 1-year retention	3	Proportion of teachers retained from the prior year
Teacher retention, teachers with less than five years of experience	1	Proportion of teachers retained from the prior year among the subset of teachers with fewer than five years' experience at the school
Non-expulsion rate	1	Fraction of students not expelled during that year
Non-suspension rate	3	Fraction of students not suspended at all during that year
Student CTE participation rate	2	Proportion of high school students participating in career and technical education courses
Percent of teachers with certifications	1	Percentage of teachers in the school who have certifications
Teacher diploma rate	1	Percentage of teachers in the school who have a teacher diploma

Table D.3
Treatment Effects for All Outcomes

Outcome	Year Effect	Coefficient	Standard Error
Math percentile scores	2nd	2.608***	0.626
Math percentile scores	3rd+	2.867***	0.706
Reading percentile scores	2nd	4.944***	0.594
Reading percentile scores	3rd+	6.219***	0.719
Science percentile scores	2nd	0.089**	0.036
Science percentile scores	3rd+	0.095***	0.029
Social studies percentile scores	2nd	3.940***	0.694
Social studies percentile scores	3rd+	3.158***	0.723
Attendance rate	2nd	0.664	11.099
Attendance rate	3rd+	0.485	6.261
Climate rating (1–5)	2nd	0.118	0.083
Climate rating (1–5)	3rd+	0.000	0.000
Principal's average climate rating (1–4)	2nd	0.055**	0.028
Principal's average climate rating (1–4)	3rd+	0.047	0.040
Principal's rating of overall school climate (1–4)	2nd	0.292***	0.068
Principal's rating of overall school climate (1–4)	3rd+	0.175**	0.072
Teacher's average climate rating (1–4)	2nd	−0.062***	0.017
Teacher's average climate rating (1–4)	3rd+	0.026	0.023
Teacher's rating of overall school climate (1–4)	2nd	−0.054***	0.015
Teacher's rating of overall school climate (1–4)	3rd+	0.011	0.030
Graduation rate	2nd	1.004	0.729
Graduation rate	3rd+	1.267	1.239
Principal retention (2 years)	2nd	5.781***	1.982
Principal retention (3 years)	3rd+	7.805**	3.107
Teacher 1-year retention	2nd	0.020	0.398
Teacher 1-year retention	3rd+	1.268***	0.447
Teacher retention, teachers < five years' experience	2nd	−3.122*	1.629
Teacher retention, teachers < five years' experience	3rd+	−11.010***	1.887
Non-expulsion rate	2nd	−0.008	0.010

Table D.3—continued

Outcome	Year Effect	Coefficient	Standard Error
Non-expulsion rate	3rd+	0.018	0.017
Non-suspension rate	2nd	1.331	1.134
Non-suspension rate	3rd+	−0.150	2.133
Student CTE participation rate	2nd	-1.594	5.338
Student CTE participation rate	3rd+	−2.546	23.422
Percent of teachers with certifications	2nd	0.087***	0.008
Percent of teachers with certifications	3rd+	0.119***	0.009
Teacher diploma rate	2nd	0.002	0.023
Teacher diploma rate	3rd+	−0.001	0.021

NOTES: * p < 0.1, ** p < 0.05, *** p < 0.01.

Table D.4
Regressions of School Achievement Treatment Effects on PPI Components

PPI Component	All	Reassigned Principals	New District Hires	Univariate Regressions
Leader standards	−1.688	−9.572	1.806	2.591***
	(3.544)	(6.630)	(3.721)	(0.983)
Residency	−2.261	1.563	−3.402**	−2.369**
	(1.402)	(4.072)	(1.664)	(1.059)
Preferred preservice	0.359	−0.480	1.196	−1.366
	(1.196)	(2.577)	(1.421)	(0.916)
Talent pool	−2.567*	−1.401	−2.482	−2.387
	(1.547)	(3.191)	(1.907)	(1.477)
Evaluation	4.301	13.45**	0.723	2.732***
	(3.594)	(6.502)	(3.807)	(0.998)
Induction PD	−2.003	−7.518*	−2.719*	−2.465**
	(1.273)	(4.447)	(1.480)	(1.223)
Induction mentoring	0.0694	−4.059	1.146	−0.0698
	(1.109)	(2.724)	(1.376)	(1.070)
Talent pool score				0.861*
				(0.452)
Observations	925	163	762	—
R-squared	0.226	0.161	0.222	—

NOTES: Standard errors in parentheses. * p < 0.1, ** p < 0.05, *** p < 0.01.

of residency programs after controlling for participation in a preparation program run by a preferred preservice provider. That effect is identified primarily based on variation among principals within one of the PPI districts. Further research is warranted to better understand the role of residency-based experiences in districts undertaking PPI-type reforms. The univariate regressions reveal a positive association between adoption of leader standards and new evaluation systems among PPI districts and PPI effects. They also suggest a positive relationship between a principal's talent pool score and PPI effects on achievement. We observe a negative correlation between induction PD and residency based preservice and PPI effects in the univariate regressions, as well.

We also separately evaluated component mechanism effects via subgroup regressions by estimating the primary regression model separately on all treated principals who had a given component (e.g., was from a talent pool) and those who did not, to contrast them. The findings from that analysis, while not reported here, were not always in the same direction as these regressions, but typically had small differences between the two and overlapping confidence intervals, further suggesting the scarcity of clear findings related to outsized effects from particular components of the pipeline in isolation. This leads us to have less confidence in our findings in this area, because they are not robust to diverse specifications.

Table D.5 shows the same regressions with pipeline components, but now looking at principal retention treatment effects. We again find few strong or consistent patterns. The clearest results indicate a positive association between new principals' experiences of induction PD and a higher likelihood of staying in their job after hire, which appears to be stronger among reassigned principals.

Table D.5
Regressions of School Principal Retention Treatment Effects on Principal Pipeline Components

	All	Reassigned Principals	New District Hires	Univariate Regressions
Leader standards	0.00774	0.0659	−0.0210	−0.0274
	(0.102)	(0.327)	(0.0985)	(0.0330)
Residency	0.0104	0.0149	0.0445	0.0389
	(0.0442)	(0.132)	(0.0496)	(0.0335)
Preferred preservice	0.0374	0.206*	0.0125	0.0394
	(0.0371)	(0.106)	(0.0419)	(0.0283)
Talent Pool	−0.0318	−0.00721	−0.130*	−0.0510
	(0.0648)	(0.257)	(0.0678)	(0.0570)
Evaluation	−0.0387	−0.0982	0.00876	−0.0305
	(0.106)	(0.322)	(0.105)	(0.0336)
Induction PD	0.0326	0.173	0.0192	0.0389
	(0.0363)	(0.142)	(0.0390)	(0.0362)
Induction mentoring	0.0626*	0.154***	0.0601	0.0550*
	(0.0330)	(0.0577)	(0.0423)	(0.0326)
Talent pool score				−0.0138
				(0.0253)
Observations	867	143	724	—
R-squared	0.074	0.149	0.076	—

NOTES: Standard errors in parentheses. * $p < 0.1$, ** $p < 0.05$, *** $p < 0.01$.

References

Allen, D. G., P. C. Bryant, and J. M. Vardaman, "Retaining Talent: Replacing Misconceptions with Evidence-Based Strategies," *Academy of Management Perspectives*, Vol. 24, No. 2, May 2010.

Anderson, Leslie M., Brenda J. Turnbull, and Erikson R. Arcaira, *Leader Tracking Systems: Turning Data into Information for School Leadership*, Washington, D.C.: Policy Studies Associates, 2017.

Anderson, Leslie M., and Brenda J. Turnbull, *Evaluating and Supporting Principals*, Washington, D.C.: Policy Studies Associates, 2016.

Anderson, Leslie M., and Brenda J. Turnbull, *Sustaining a Principal Pipeline*, Washington, D.C.: Policy Studies Associates, 2016.

Bang, H., and Robins, J. M., "Doubly Robust Estimation in Missing Data and Causal Inference Models," *Biometrics*, Vol. 61, No. 4, 2005, pp. 962–973.

Branch, G. F., E. A. Hanushek, and S. G. Rivkin, *Estimating the Effect of Leaders on Public Sector Productivity: The Case of School Principals*, Washington, D.C.: National Center for Analysis of Longitudinal Data in Education Research, Working Paper 66, 2012. As of October 2014: http://ideas.repec.org/p/nbr/nberwo/17803.html

Cascio, Wayne F., "The Economic Impact of Employee Behaviors on Organizational Performance," *California Management Review*, Vol. 48, No. 4, Summer 2006, pp. 41–59.

Clark, D., P. Martorell, and J. Rockoff, *School Principals and School Performance*, Washington, D.C.: The Urban Institute, Working Paper No. 38, 2009.

Clark, M. A., H. S. Chiang, T. Silva, S. McConnell, K. Sonnenfeld, A. Erbe, and M. Puma, *The Effectiveness of Secondary Math Teachers from Teach For America and the Teaching Fellows Programs*, Washington, D.C.: National Center for Education Evaluation and Regional Assistance, Institute of Education Sciences, U.S. Department of Education, NCEE 2013-4015, 2013.

Coelli, M., and D. A. Green, "Leadership Effects: School Principals and Student Outcomes," *Economics of Education Review*, Vol. 31, No. 1, 2012, pp. 92–109.

Cowan, J., and D. Goldhaber, "National Board Certification and Teacher Effectiveness: Evidence from Washington State," *Journal of Research on Educational Effectiveness*, Vol. 9, No. 3, 2016, pp. 233–258.

Curtis, Rachel E., and Judy Wurtzel, eds., *Teaching Talent: A Visionary Framework for Human Capital in Education*, Cambridge, Mass.: Harvard Education Press, 2010.

Darling-Hammond, Linda, Michelle LaPointe, Debra Meyerson, Margaret Terry Orr, and Carol Cohen, *Preparing School Leaders for a Changing World: Lessons from Exemplary Leadership Development Programs—Final Report*, Stanford, Calif.: Stanford University, Stanford Educational Leadership Institute, 2007. As of August 9, 2017: https://www.wallacefoundation.org/knowledge-center/Documents/Preparing-School-Leaders.pdf

Education Week Research Center, *Indicator Definition: High-Minority*, 2018. As of August 6, 2018: http://www.edcounts.org/indicatorDefinition.php?id=597

Engdahl, T., "Grant Will Help DPS Take Next LEAP," *Chalkbeat*, July 25, 2013. As of October 23, 2018: https://chalkbeat.org/posts/co/2013/07/25/grant-will-help-dps-take-next-leap/

Gates, Susan M., Matthew D. Baird, Christopher Joseph Doss, Linda S. Hamilton, Isaac M. Opper, Benjamin K. Master, Andrea Prado Tuma, Mirka Vuollo, and Melanie A. Zaber, *Preparing School Leaders for Success: Evaluation of New Leaders' Aspiring Principals Program 2012–2017*, Santa Monica, Calif.: RAND Corporation, RR-2812-NL, 2019. As of February 13, 2019: http://www.rand.org/pubs/research_reports/RR2812.html

George W. Bush Institute, *A Framework for Principal Talent Management*, Dallas, Tex., October 2016. As of August 9, 2018: http://gwbcenter.imgix.net/Resources/gwbi-framework-principal-talent-mgmt.pdf

Gill, Jennifer, *Chock Full of Data: How School Districts Are Building Leader Tracking Systems to Support Principal Pipelines*, New York: The Wallace Foundation, July 2016. As of May 23, 2017: http://www.wallacefoundation.org/knowledge-center/Pages/Chock-Full-of-Data-How-School-Districts-Are-Building-Leader-Tracking-Systems-to-Support-Principal-Pipelines.aspx

Grissom, J. A., and B. Bartanen, "Principal Effectiveness and Principal Turnover," *Education Finance and Policy*, advance online publication, 2018. As of November 30, 2018: https://www.mitpressjournals.org/doi/abs/10.1162/edfp_a_00256

Grissom, J. A., R. S. Blissett, and H. Mitani, "Evaluating School Principals: Supervisor Ratings of Principal Practice and Principal Job Performance," *Educational Evaluation and Policy Analysis*, Vol. 40, No. 3, 2018, pp. 446–472.

Grissom, J. A., D. Kalogrides, and S. Loeb, "Using Student Test Scores to Measure Principal Performance," *Education Evaluation and Policy Analysis*, Vol. 37, No. 1, 2015, pp. 3–28.

Haberman, M., "Principal CEO," *HuffPost*, February 15, 2011. As of May 5, 2017: http://www.huffingtonpost.com/Michael-Haberman/principal-cco_b_823375.html

Herman, Rebecca, Susan M. Gates, Aziza Arifkhanova, Mark Barrett, Andriy Bega, Emilio R. Chavez-Herrerias, Eugeniu Han, Mark Harris, Katya Migacheva, Rachel Ross, Jennifer T. Leschitz, and Stephani L. Wrabel, *School Leadership Interventions Under the Every Student Succeeds Act: Evidence Review—Updated and Expanded*, Santa Monica, Calif.: RAND Corporation, RR-1550-3-WF, 2017. As of August 10, 2018: http://www.rand.org/pubs/research_reports/RR1550-3.html

Huselid, M. A., B. E. Becker, and R. W. Beatty, *The Workforce Scorecard: Managing Human Capital to Execute Strategy*, Boston, Mass.: Harvard Business School Press, 2005.

Iacus, S. M., G. King, and G. Porro, "Causal Inference Without Balance Checking: Coarsened Exact Matching," *Political Analysis*, Vol. 20, No. 1, 2012, pp. 1–24.

Jacob, R., C. Armstrong, and J. Willard, *Mobilizing Volunteer Tutors to Improve Student Literacy: Implementation, Impacts, and Costs of the Reading Partners Program*, Oakland, Calif.: MDRC, 2015.

Kane, T. J., D. F. McCaffrey, T. Miller, and D. O. Staiger, *Have We Identified Effective Teachers? Validating Measures of Effective Teaching Using Random Assignment*, Seattle, Wash.: Bill and Melinda Gates Foundation, Measures of Effective Teaching project research paper, January 2013.

Kaufman, Julia H., Susan M. Gates, Melody Harvey, Yanlin Wang, and Mark Barrett, *What It Takes to Operate and Maintain Principal Pipelines: Costs and Other Resources*, Santa Monica, Calif.: RAND Corporation, RR-2078-WF, 2017. As of June 13, 2018:
http://www.rand.org/pubs/research_reports/RR2078.html

Kim, J. S., J. Guryan, T. G. White, D. M. Quinn, L. Capotosto, and H. C. Kingston, "Delayed Effects of a Low-Cost and Large-Scale Summer Reading Intervention on Elementary School Children's Reading Comprehension," *Journal of Research on Educational Effectiveness*, Vol. 9, Suppl. 1, 2016, pp. 1–22.

Korach, S., and S. Cosner, "Developing the Leadership Pipeline: Comprehensive Leadership Development," in M. D. Young and G. M. Crow, eds., *Handbook of Research on the Education of School Leaders*, New York: Routledge, 2017, pp. 262–282.

Lawler, Edward E., III, *Strategic Talent Management: Lessons from the Corporate World*, Madison, Wisc.: University of Wisconsin–Madison, Wisconsin Center for Education Research, Consortium for Policy Research in Education (CPRE), 2008.

Leithwood, L., K. Seashore Louis, S. Anderson, and K. Wahlstrom, *How Leadership Influences Student Learning*, New York: The Wallace Foundation, 2004.

Miller, A., "Principal Turnover and Student Achievement," *Economics of Education Review*, Vol. 36, No. C, 2013, pp. 60–72.

National Academies of Sciences, Engineering, and Medicine, *Advancing the Power of Economic Evidence to Inform Investments in Children, Youth, and Families*, Washington, D.C.: National Academies Press, 2016.

National Center for Education Statistics, "ElSi: Elementary/Secondary Information System," undated. As of May 24, 2017:
https://nces.ed.gov/ccd/elsi/

National Center for Education Statistics, "Enrollment, Poverty and Federal Funds for the 100 Largest School Districts, by Enrollment Size in 2012: Selected Years 2011–12 Through 2014," *Digest of Education Statistics*, Table 215.30, Washington, D.C., May 2015. As of August 10, 2018:
https://nces.ed.gov/programs/digest/d14/tables/dt14_215.30.asp

NCES—*See* National Center for Education Statistics.

New York City Leadership Academy and American Institutes for Research, *Ready to Lead: Designing Residencies for Better Principal Preparation*, New York: New York City Leadership Academy, 2016. As of November 1, 2018:
https://live-nyc-leadership-academy.pantheonsite.io/wp-content/uploads/2018/07/ready-to-lead-residency-guide.pdf

Public Law 114-95, Every Student Succeeds Act, December 10, 2015.

Rangel, Virginia Snodgrass, "A Review of the Literature on Principal Turnover," *Review of Educational Research*, Vol. 88, No. 1, 2018, pp. 87–124.

School Leaders Network, *Churn: The High Cost of Principal Turnover*, Hinsdale, Mass., 2014.

Sokol, M., "Sticker Shock: How Hillsborough County's Gates Grant Became a Budget Buster," *Tampa Bay Times*, October 23, 2015 (updated December 15, 2015). As of October 23, 2018:
https://www.tampabay.com/news/education/k12/sticker-shock-how-hillsborough-countys-gates-grant-became-a-budget-buster/2250988

Stecher, Brian M., Deborah J. Holtzman, Michael S. Garet, Laura S. Hamilton, John Engberg, Elizabeth D. Steiner, Abby Robyn, Matthew D. Baird, Italo A. Gutierrez, Evan D. Peet, Iliana Brodziak de los Reyes, Kaitlin Fronberg, Gabriel Weinberger, Gerald Paul Hunter, and Jay Chambers, *Improving Teaching Effectiveness Final Report: The Intensive Partnerships for Effective Teaching Through 2015–2016*, Santa Monica, Calif.: RAND Corporation, RR-2242-BMGF, 2018. As of July 9, 2018:
https://www.rand.org/pubs/research_reports/RR2242.html

Torres, Z., "Denver Public Schools Gets $10 Million Grant from Gates Foundation," *Denver Post*, July 24, 2013 (updated April 29, 2016). As of October 23, 2018:
https://www.denverpost.com/2013/07/24/
denver-public-schools-gets-10-million-grant-from-gates-foundation/

Turnbull, Brenda J., Leslie M. Anderson, Derek L. Riley, Jaclyn R. MacFarlane, and Daniel K. Aladjem, *The Principal Pipeline Initiative in Action*, Washington, D.C.: Policy Studies Associates, 2016.

Turnbull, Brenda J., Derek L. Riley, Erikson R. Arcaira, Leslie M. Anderson, and Jaclyn R. MacFarlane, *Six Districts Begin the Principal Pipeline Initiative*, Washington, D.C.: Policy Studies Associates, 2013.

Turnbull, Brenda J., Derek L. Riley, and Jaclyn R. MacFarlane, *Cultivating Talent Through a Principal Pipeline*, Washington, D.C.: Policy Studies Associates, 2013.

Turnbull, Brenda J., Derek L. Riley, and Jaclyn R. MacFarlane, *Districts Taking Charge of the Principal Pipeline*, Washington, D.C.: Policy Studies Associates, 2015.

Tuttle, C. C., P. Gleason, V. Knechtel, I. Nichols-Barrer, K. Booker, G. Chojnacki, T. Coen, and L. Goble, *Understanding the Effect of KIPP as It Scales*, Vol. 1: *Impacts on Achievement and Other Outcomes*, Washington, D.C.: Mathematica Policy Research, 2015.

U.S. Department of Education, *Status and Trends in the Education of Racial and Ethnic Minorities*, Washington, D.C., NCES 2007-039, 2007, p. 23. As of August 6 2018:
https://nces.ed.gov/pubs2007/2007039.pdf

U.S. Department of Education, *Fundamental Change: Innovation in America's Schools Under Race to the Top*, Washington, D.C., 2015. As of November 13 2018:
https://www2.ed.gov/programs/racetothetop/rttfinalrpt1115.pdf

U.S. Department of Education, Institute of Education Sciences, National Center for Education Evaluation and Regional Assistance, *WWC Intervention Report: Teach for America*, 2016. As of November 14, 2018:
https://ies.ed.gov/ncee/wwc/Docs/InterventionReports/wwc_tfa_083116.pdf

U.S. Department of Education, *Principal Attrition and Mobility: Results from the 2016–17 Principal Follow-Up Survey First Look*, Washington, D.C., NCES 2018-066, 2018a. As of August 6, 2018:
https://nces.ed.gov/pubs2018/2018066.pdf

U.S. Department of Education, *The Condition of Education 2018*, Washington, D.C., NCES 2018-144, 2018b. As of August 6, 2018:
https://nces.ed.gov/pubs2018/2018144.pdf

U.S. Department of Education, Institute of Education Sciences, National Center for Education Evaluation and Regional Assistance, *WWC Intervention Report: Knowledge Is Power Program (KIPP)*, Washington, D.C., 2018c. As of November 14, 2018:
https://ies.ed.gov/ncee/wwc/Docs/InterventionReports/wwc_kipp_012318.pdf

Wakefield, N., A. Abbatiello, D. Agarwal, K. Pastakia, and A. van Berkel, "Leadership Awakened: Generations, Teams, Science," in *2016 Global Human Capital Trends: Different by Design*, Westlake, Tex.: Deloitte University Press, February 26, 2016. As of May 5, 2017: https://www2.deloitte.com/content/dam/Deloitte/be/Documents/human-capital/gx-dup-global-human-capital-trends-2016.pdf

Wallace Foundation, "Knowledge Center: Building a Stronger Principalship," undated. As of August 9, 2018: https://www.wallacefoundation.org/knowledge-center/pages/building-a-stronger-principalship.aspx

Wallace Foundation, *Request for Proposals: Building a Better Principal Pipeline to Boost Student Achievement: A Wallace Demonstration Project with Districts and Principal Training Programs*, New York: The Wallace Foundation, 2011.

Wallace Foundation, "Wallace Invests $30 Million to Strengthen Supervisors of School Principals to Improve Their Ability to Lead Schools," press release, June 24, 2014. As of August 9, 2018: https://www.wallacefoundation.org/news-and-media/press-releases/pages/wallace-invests-$30-million-to-strengthen-supervisors.aspx